Making A Difference

....

Using Sociology to Create a Better World

MICHAEL SCHWALBE
NORTH CAROLINA STATE UNIVERSITY

New York　　Oxford
OXFORD UNIVERSITY PRESS

Oxford University Press is a department of the University of Oxford.
It furthers the University's objective of excellence in research, scholarship,
and education by publishing worldwide. Oxford is a registered trade mark of
Oxford University Press in the UK and certain other countries.

Published in the United States of America by Oxford University Press
198 Madison Avenue, New York, NY 10016, United States of America.

Library of Congress Cataloging-in-Publication Data

Names: Schwalbe, Michael, 1956- author.
Title: Making a difference : using sociology to create a better world /
    Michael Schwalbe, North Carolina State University.
Description: New York, NY : Oxford University Press, [2020] | Includes index.
    | Identifiers: LCCN 2018045544 (print) | LCCN 2018046882 (ebook) |
    ISBN 9780190927219 (e-book) | ISBN 9780190927202 (pbk.)
Subjects: LCSH: Sociology. | Applied sociology. | Social change.
Classification: LCC HM585 (ebook) | LCC HM585 .S377 2020 (print) |
    DDC 301–dc23
LC record available at https://lccn.loc.gov/2018045544

9 8 7 6 5 4 3 2 1

Printed by Sheridan Books, Inc., United States of America

TABLE OF CONTENTS
....

....

CHAPTER 1

Introduction

Sociology and Social Change

The question usually arises about halfway through every semester. It's tinged with frustration and goes something like this: *sociology tells us what's wrong with society, but what does sociology say we should do about it?* Most people who teach sociology courses have probably heard a version of this question. A lot of students who've taken sociology courses have probably sought an answer. I'm going to offer one. More than one, actually.

When I've been asked the question, I've usually said that, yes, it can be discouraging to hear so much about what's wrong with society, but this is information we can't do without. Before we try to change society, we need to know how society works so that our efforts to fix things are effective and don't make matters worse. I've said that sociology can provide this kind of knowledge to activists and legislators who want to make the world a better place. So it's up to us as citizens, I've said, to figure out how to use the knowledge that sociology provides, and that falling into a funk because the world is imperfect isn't a constructive response.

Other sociology professors have probably given much the same answer. And it's not a bad answer, as far as it goes. Anyone who agrees that it's wise to have a good analysis of a problem before jumping in and trying to solve it will appreciate the data and insight that sociology (and other social sciences) can offer. Yet the answer that invokes sociology's practical value for diagnosing and solving social problems rarely satisfies, because, even though it's true, it comes across as too abstract, too lofty. A better answer, I think, is one that connects sociology to what can be done differently in everyday life.

Most people—and I'm thinking primarily of students in college and university classrooms—who ask about sociology's value as a guide to action are not policymakers (though some will become policymakers) or activists (though some are, and some will become activists). They are just people who want to know how to use the knowledge they are acquiring to make a difference in the world. I think it should be possible to provide an answer that doesn't imply the need to join a social movement or get elected to office or become a professor. As I will explain, there are many ways to use sociology to make the world a better place—ways that don't require extraordinary measures, just thoughtful practices that anyone can adopt.

The practices I'm going to describe grow out of three things: a body of knowledge that sociology has created over the years, a set of methods that sociologists use to study the social world, and what I call "sociological mindfulness." It's not that sociological knowledge, methods, or mindfulness can tell us precisely what to do to change the world in a particular way. If this were the case, sociology already would have solved the world's problems. What sociology provides, more humbly, is a set of resources—information, ideas, methods of investigation, ways of thinking—that can help us figure out what to do to help make the world a better place.

So what does it mean to make the world a better place? Better for whom? Better in what ways?

When students ask about the practical value of sociology, they already have in mind, at least implicitly, a better world. This would be a world in which the problems that sociology makes visible—racism, sexism, discrimination, poverty, violence, disease, inequality, oppression, exploitation—don't exist. Such a world would be better in the sense that those who now suffer injustice and various forms of indignity, misery, and deprivation would no longer suffer in these ways. Many people, not just college students, would probably accept this vision of what a better world would look like. It certainly strikes me as a good vision.

Yet here is where things get sticky because one person's problem can be another person's solution. For example, low wages are a problem for workers trying to earn a decent living; but low wages are a solution for capitalists trying to increase profits. War is a problem for people whose bodies and lives are destroyed by it; but it's a solution for those seeking power over others. Discrimination is a problem for people in marginalized groups; but it's a solution for people in dominant groups who want to protect their advantages. What these examples imply is that there is bound to be dispute over what constitutes a better world, especially when the starting point is a society fraught with inequalities. People who benefit from these inequalities might not want to change society to make the world better for someone else.

As I said, I find the vision of a world without racism, sexism, discrimination, poverty, violence, disease, inequality, oppression, and exploitation appealing. I think this would indeed be a better world, and I hope that people of goodwill would agree. But it's important not to equate "better world" with utopia. Better just means improved, not rebuilt to perfection. For now, a better world, as I see it, is one in which there is more opportunity and less discrimination, more peace and less violence, more equality and less poverty, more democracy and less domination, more joy and less suffering. Nudging the world in these directions is doable, and sociology can guide anyone who wants to add their strength to the effort.

In the chapters ahead, I'll draw on sociological knowledge—by which I mean claims about the social world that we have good research-based reasons to believe are true—to propose actions that readers can take if they would like to make the world a better place in the ways noted above. I'll also draw on what sociologists know about how to study the social world and produce valid knowledge about it. As I'll show, the principles and methods of sociological research can be useful guides to action in everyday life and not just in the context of doing science. But what is perhaps even more useful, when it comes to bringing sociology to bear on everyday life, is sociological mindfulness. The idea of sociological mindfulness is going to be central to much of what else I say in this book, and so I need to devote some pages to explaining it.

Sociological Mindfulness

In the mid-1990s, I decided to write a book about how to think sociologically. My inspiration came from two classics in this genre: C. Wright Mills's *The Sociological Imagination* and Peter Berger's *Invitation to Sociology*. I wanted to convey many of the lessons that I had learned from Mills and Berger (and other writers) but do it in a way that was more accessible and personal, and more about what people saw and experienced in everyday life. I also wanted to say how thinking sociologically could make a difference in one's life. I had been writing along these lines for years, mostly in the form of handouts for my students. It seemed like it was time to put these thoughts into a book and share them more widely.

But writing a book is harder than writing handouts. And so after a little while, I got stuck. I reviewed my notes, started again, and got bogged down again. I couldn't find a guiding thread to keep the book on track. I tried elaborating Mills's concept of the sociological imagination, but the farther I went down that road, the less I liked the connotations of "imagination." I even tried writing in different voices—friendly teacher, clever social observer, hard-boiled scientist, curmudgeonly professor. Nothing felt right, at least not for long.

Around the same time, I was reading a book by a Buddhist teacher, Thich Nhat Hanh, and discovered the concept of mindfulness. In Buddhist thought, and today in some branches of Western psychology, "mindfulness" refers to nonjudgmental, meditative paying attention—sometimes to one's own body, sometimes to one's surroundings. It occurred to me that thinking sociologically is a special kind of paying attention to the social world, a form of heightened awareness. Thinking sociologically can be described, in other words, as a kind of mindfulness. This was the idea, the guiding thread, I needed to find my way forward.

The book I eventually wrote is called *The Sociologically Examined Life*, which was first published in 1998 and is now in its fifth edition (Oxford, 2018). In the book, I explain all the ways of paying attention to the social world that constitute being sociologically mindful. I can't tuck that whole book into a few pages here, but I can review the ideas that are most pertinent to creating social change. I should say, too, that there is nothing especially Buddhist about this perspective. What it's about is heeding the ancient Greek admonitions, often associated with Socrates and Plato, to examine our lives and seek to know ourselves, albeit in a sociological way.

Mindfulness of the Social World as Humanly Made

If there is a first step in being sociologically mindful, it is learning to see the social world as humanly made. Because we are all born into pre-existing groups—families, communities, societies, nations—with established cultures and ways of doing things, it can seem like the social world is just there, a reality as hard as a mountain range or as independent of human will as the weather. But this is not really so. All parts of the social world—all the groups, organizations, institutions, political and economic systems; all our beliefs, values, symbols, and practices—were created, once upon a time, by people.

It might seem obvious that the social world is created by people. Where else would it come from? Yet we often experience it as apart from us, or over and above us. This experience is reflected in how we talk about the social world. We say that the *market* did this or that, or that the *economy* did this or that, or that *technology* drives change, or that *globalization* is transforming society, and so on. When we think about and talk about the social world in this way—as if it were made of things and forces that are independent of human action—we subtly reinforce the idea that it is unchangeable and that what we do doesn't matter.

Being sociologically mindful means, in part, recognizing that the social world is humanly made and paying attention to how this occurs. When people invent new concepts and ideas, when they share new ideas with others, when they create new groups and organizations, when they build new tools and technologies, when they come up with new ways of doing things together, when they devise new laws and policies, and when they reject old ways of thinking—they are changing the social world. So while it might seem that the social world is as solid and steady as a mountain range, in fact it's changing all the time, and we participate in this process, to some degree, every day. Being sociologically mindful thus allows us to see more possibilities for change, more possibilities for making a difference, than we might have imagined.

Mindfulness of Interdependence

Practicing sociological mindfulness also means paying attention to interdependence. In Western societies, especially the United States, we tend to think of ourselves as making our way through life as individuals. We are of course individuals in the sense that each of us is a discrete organism in which a single mind has emerged. Yet this singularity can be exaggerated to the point of obscuring our interdependence with others. Were it not for this interdependence, we could not even become self-conscious creatures.

As infants and young children, our survival depends on the adults who feed and care for us. Our ability to think in human ways—to name and understand the things of the world, including ourselves—depends on learning to use the language spoken by those around us. We also learn from others how to behave in proper ways so that we can avoid trouble and get along in the world. Unlike other animals, very little adaptive behavior is hardwired into us; we need to learn, from the examples and instruction of others, how to participate competently in social life.

The advanced skills of reading and writing, thinking logically, and interpreting complex information also grow out of our interactions with others. We might acquire these skills more or less quickly, but we wouldn't acquire them at all if not for the people who teach us. Having acquired literacy and reasoning skills, we can absorb the lessons of history, science, philosophy, and art. All this social input is what makes us who and what we are. Being sociologically mindful, we thus see that our individuality is not natural or inevitable; it is a result of the experiences we have as members of a community. It is a result, in other words, of our interdependence with others.

Adult achievement is no less a result of interdependence. Getting ahead in any modern society depends on organizations and institutions. One can't become a university professor if there are no universities; one can't become a judge if there is no legal system; one can't become a corporate executive if there are no corporations; one can't become a movie star if there is no film industry. No matter how strenuous our individual efforts, we can't get ahead alone; every path we take and every place we strive to reach exists only by virtue of the organized efforts of many other people.

Life in modern societies also depends on a great deal of infrastructure—roads, bridges, public schools and universities, public hospitals, mass transit systems, airports, seaports, libraries, parks, water and sewage plants, energy utilities, police and fire departments, courts, governments—which is built and maintained by pooling our resources. The organizations and material structures created through this kind of cooperation benefit everyone. But because we often take infrastructure for granted, we can easily forget how interdependent we are when it comes to being able to pursue and achieve success, or simply to live safe and comfortable lives.

Being mindful of interdependence, we see more deeply into how the social world works. We see that who we become, what we can achieve, and the conditions of our everyday lives depend on a tremendous amount of organized, collective effort in which we are enmeshed. This is a basic sociological insight, one that counters the exaggerated notions of individualism that are popular in US culture. But perhaps the more important point is this: because we are so interdependent, our actions can affect others, just as theirs can affect us. The implication is that what we do—how we choose to be enmeshed in the life of a community—can make a difference.

Mindfulness of Power

A third aspect of sociological mindfulness is paying attention to how power operates in social life. Of course, we all come to realize, well before adulthood, that power demands our attention. This is because we discover at an early age that others can control us, or try to, by dispensing rewards and punishments. We think of these others—parents, teachers, bosses, government officials—as having the power to make us do things or not do things. We also learn to avoid displeasing these powerful others so that we can get more of what we want and less of what we don't want. It would thus be fair to say that being mindful of power is a prerequisite for navigating one's way through the social world.

But being sociologically mindful of power is different from simply being aware of its existence or its impact on our lives. Being sociologically mindful of power means paying attention to its social foundations. It means, in other words, asking what the power of an individual or group is based on. If we look closely in a sociological way, what we will see is that power depends on cooperation and shared definitions of reality. Consider, for example, the power of teachers.

We think of teachers as having the power to enforce rules, assign tasks, judge student work, and give grades—actions that can affect students' lives for better or worse. This being the case, most students do what teachers ask. But it's important to recognize that this ability to compel students' behavior does not come from a force inside teachers. It comes from a system of cooperation that includes students, teachers, administrators, staff, school board members, parents, employers, social workers, and perhaps even police. If not for how all these people cooperate to "do schooling" in a particular way, teachers would have no power.

The system of cooperation that gives rise to what we call "schools" rests in turn on a set of beliefs shared by those who participate in the system. These are beliefs about what schooling is, what education is, why education is valuable, and about how teachers and students are supposed to behave. These beliefs, taken together, can be said to constitute a shared definition of reality. And, again, if not for this shared definition of reality, there would be no system of cooperation, no schools, and no teachers wielding power.

The power of bosses can be understood in the same way. Bosses have the power to enforce rules, assign tasks, judge employee work, and decide about pay and promotions. Because these actions can affect employees' lives for better or worse, most people do what their bosses tell them to do. But as with teachers, the power of bosses comes from cooperation and a shared definition of reality. If not for the cooperation of bosses with each other, with investors, with other employees, and with police and other government officials who protect property and enforce rules created by bosses, there would be no workplaces in which bosses could order people around. These networks of cooperation rest on shared beliefs about what employment is, how bosses and employees are supposed to behave, the value of jobs and money, and who can rightfully control property in what ways. Without these beliefs to guide and legitimate the forms of cooperation we call "workplaces," there would be no bosses with power.

What I have been saying about teachers and bosses applies as well to presidents and military leaders. Even with all the guns or bombs in the world, no president or general would have much power without followers willing to use those guns and bombs to hurt other people. Why would some people be willing to hurt others merely because a politician or general says so? Only because they have been taught to accept the authority of presidents and generals as legitimate. And how do such beliefs get implanted in the minds of those who would use violence? Only through the cooperative efforts of a great many people who create and transmit the ideas that violence is acceptable and obedience is obligatory.

Being sociologically mindful about how power operates in social life, we see that making others do things—what we usually think of as exercising power—always depends on the beliefs in the minds of those being told to obey or cooperate. If the beliefs that justify cooperation are challenged and begin to break down, making it hard for bosses of all kinds to mobilize others to serve them, then power fades and dies. Looking at power in this way has at least two implications for social change. One is that power can be resisted by offering new ideas that lead people to withhold cooperation. A second implication is that no arrangements that sustain the exercise of power, no matter how firm these arrangements might seem, are eternal.

Mindfulness of Inequality

A fourth aspect of sociological mindfulness is attention to inequality. As with power, we begin learning about inequality at an early age. We might learn, for example, that other children have nicer clothes and more expensive toys, and that their families have newer cars and bigger houses. We might learn that other children get fairer treatment from adults. We might learn, most likely in school, that one must compete against others and, if possible, win, because winning is how one benefits from inequality. Even if there isn't a lot of inequality right around us, we still learn from media that some people are rich and others are poor. It is hard to be awake in the modern world and not be aware, even as a young person, of the inequalities that surround us.

How, then, is being sociologically mindful about inequality different from merely being aware that it exists? First, it involves looking at how different kinds of inequalities are connected. Inequalities in income, for example, can produce disparities in education, health care, safety, and material comfort. In a capitalist society, there is nothing mysterious about these connections; everyone knows that having more money means that you can buy more goods, services, and experiences that make life pleasant and fulfilling. But other connections are harder to see.

For example, wealth—the value of all the economic assets a person owns—can be a source not only of material comfort but of psychological security. This is because wealth allows a person to live with less fear that job loss or serious illness will turn into a life-disrupting disaster. Psychological security is not visible in the way that clothes and cars and houses are visible, but it might be more important to living a good life—if we think of a good life as one free from chronic anxiety and dread. In this case, sociological mindfulness directs our attention to a connection between economic inequality and inequality in psychological well-being.

Another example is the connection between wealth and political power. Every adult citizen might be able to vote, but those with wealth can exert more influence by contributing to political candidates and elected officials. Great wealth can be a source of even more political power if it is used to buy public relations campaigns, establish think tanks, or acquire media corporations. When wealth is used in these ways—to shape public opinion and influence government—the results are usually changes in laws and policies that benefit the already wealthy and increase inequality all the more. In this case, we see a connection between economic inequality and political inequality.

Inequalities in status—a term that refers to social honor, prestige, or respect—are often linked to inequalities in wealth and political power. If some groups are held in low regard—perhaps on the basis of race, ethnicity, religion, gender, or sexuality—then members of such groups might be excluded from opportunities for economic or political advancement. Being sociologically mindful means paying attention to how inequalities in status might underlie discriminatory practices that in turn produce inequalities in wealth and power. This doesn't mean assuming that such practices exist; it means looking to see if they exist and, if so, trying to understand how they work.

Another part of being sociologically mindful about inequality is paying attention to how it can affect people's well-being in non-obvious ways. I already suggested one way this can occur: a lack of wealth can undermine feelings of security. Another non-obvious consequence becomes apparent if we consider how we are usually taught in US culture to think about achievement and about where we end up in society's hierarchies of wealth, status, and power.

The usual message is that where we end up in society is a result of talent, ambition, and effort. If this is true, then people end up pretty much where they belong; the worst sink to the bottom, the mediocre fill the middle, and the best rise to the top. Because we are taught to think about inequality in this way—as the outcome of natural differences between individuals—people who fail to get ahead, or get as far ahead as they would like, tend to blame themselves. We might want to consider, however, whether this self-blame is warranted or whether it is an unfairly damaging result of how inequality is legitimated.

We can work toward an answer by noting several things, none of which should be controversial. First, some people are born into families that can give their children the resources—money, knowledge, skills, network ties—needed to do well in school and the job market; while other people are born into families that can provide far fewer, if any, of these resources. So, from the start, the race to get ahead is not a fair one. Some people, through no merit of their own, are much better equipped to compete than others. In fact, some—those born into the richest families—are so well equipped that they don't have to compete at all. They've won at birth.

Second, even though success in school can be a path to upward mobility for some people, schools themselves are not equal (in funding and staffing) and do not provide everyone with an equal education. Here again, if we look across all schools, we see that some students get more and better resources with which to compete. Moreover, schools do not treat all students the same—those from middle- and upper-middle-class homes tend to be given more help and encouragement, often in subtle ways. And third, there simply aren't enough high-status, high-paying jobs for everyone who aspires to one, in which case a lot of people aren't going to get ahead no matter how smart they are or how hard they try.

What these points suggest is that where a person ends up in society's hierarchies of wealth, status, and power is not simply a result of individual qualities or efforts but of social processes and circumstances over which no individual has much control. By implication, it is wrong and unfair to tell people that achievement depends solely, or largely, on talent, ambition, and effort, and that they have only themselves to blame for not getting ahead. Being sociologically mindful of how inequality is reproduced helps to dispel the debilitating self-blame that is created by popular ideas about achievement. A further consequence is that people may come to see themselves not as having failed but as having been failed by a system that unequally distributes opportunity.

I have already begun to touch on a third part of paying attention to inequality in a sociologically mindful way: seeing inequality as an outcome of how society is organized and the rules by which it operates. This means looking at more than where people end up in social hierarchies. It means stepping back and looking at how inequality, in society as a whole, is created and sustained by laws, policies, and bureaucratic procedures—the rules of the game, so to speak.

These rules concern such things as taxes, contracts, ownership and control of property, contributions to political campaigns, lobbying, international trade, voting, employment and discrimination, union organizing, policing, and government spending. These rules usually operate in the background of everyday life. Most people don't spend a lot of time thinking about laws concerning campaign contributions, international trade, intellectual property, or voting. But these laws greatly affect the balance of power in society, profits, wages, and the overall distribution of wealth. So while it might not seem exciting, there is no way to understand inequality without paying attention to how these laws and policies are made, interpreted, and enforced.

Although the prospect of reducing inequality can seem daunting when we consider all the rules of the game that work to preserve inequality, there is another way of looking at the situation. If inequality is a result of laws, policies, and procedures, then reducing or eliminating inequality doesn't require human or societal perfection. All it requires is doing what we already know how to do: make new laws, policies, and procedures. If the rules of a game harm most of the people who are caught in the game, the solution is to change the rules. Being sociologically mindful about inequality—seeing how it arises from the rules by which society operates—implies the possibility of change, despite claims that there is no alternative to the status quo.

Mindfulness of Process

Understanding prospects for social change depends, finally, on mindfulness of the social world as made up of processes. For ease of expression, we often talk about organizations—universities, banks, armies, hospitals, corporations—and institutions—higher education, government, the family, the market—as *things*, but these "things" are really just people interacting in patterned ways on a regular basis. One kind of pattern we call a university, another kind we call a bank, another kind we call a corporation, another kind we call a sports team, and so on. This way of looking at organizations and institutions reminds us that changing the social world does not mean trying to take down a mountain range or fill in the ocean with a shovel. It means changing the patterned ways in which we do things together, and this is a much more doable kind of project.

Being mindful of process helps us see that inequality is not the result of mysterious forces. We can look at how resources are transmitted in families; how skills and self-confidence are nurtured (or not) in schools; how people gain access to (or are excluded from) the networks through which information and opportunities are obtained; how gatekeepers and bosses make decisions about employees; how changes in the economy expand or diminish opportunities; how rules of the game are made, interpreted, and enforced. Behind every unequal outcome there is a process that can be analyzed by answering *How?* questions. If we understand these processes, we're in a better position to try to change them.

Several times I've used the image of a mountain range to suggest something big and solid—the opposite of a squishy process. But as any geologist will tell you, mountains are part of processes, too. They rise when tectonic plates push together and decline as wind and snow and rain wear them down. We don't normally see this happen because it takes millions of years, and human lives are relatively short. The same principle applies to the social world. As with mountains, the social world, though it appears stable from day to day, is changing all the time. This happens because we are always jointly engaged in learning, problem-solving, inventing, and figuring out better ways to do things together. If we are mindful of these processes, we realize that what's constant in human social life is not fixity but change.

Being sociologically mindful in the ways I've described here—paying attention to the social world as humanly made; paying attention to interdependence, power, inequality, and process—helps us see that making a difference is possible. Because the social world is always being made and remade through our actions and through the ideas we share with others, what we do—how we participate in this process—matters. We can't change the social world by ourselves overnight, but anything we choose to do differently changes our immediate social environment and has the potential to ripple outward and lead to wider changes. So what should we do to make the world better? That's the question I'm going to try to answer in the rest of this book.

Creating a Path

Even though I've said that sociological knowledge, methods, and mindfulness can guide efforts to create a better world, there are no formulas or recipes that ensure good results all the time. There are only practices, informed by sociology, that are likely to make the world a better rather than a worse place. It is these practices—actions that can be taken in everyday life—that I am going to describe in the chapters ahead. What this will amount to is not so much a map as a set of suggestions for finding or creating a path.

If you have hiked through woods or wilderness areas, you probably have a feeling for the meaning of "path." A path is a passageway through a terrain full of obstacles—trees, rocks, boulders, brush. You know, too, that a path can be more or less clear, more or less steep, more or less smooth, more or less direct. Because of these variations, a path suitable for one person might not be suitable for another. The same things are true of paths to making a difference.

There are surely obstacles: those who resist change because they benefit enormously from the status quo; those who resist change because they fear it could lead to something worse; the rewards that come from obedience and conformity; the comfort and security that come from not questioning dominant ideas; ingrained habits of mind and behavior. Getting past these obstacles can be more or less difficult at times, more or less risky, more or less costly. And what works at one time, or for one person, might not work at another time or for another person. Just like getting through the woods.

Finding or creating a path can also require exploration. The best path is not always clear from the start. It might be necessary to try one path, then another, and perhaps another before finding a way that will get you where you want to go. This too applies to both the woods and the social world. So if one path suggested by sociological knowledge, methods, or mindfulness doesn't seem to work, try another. I suppose it's possible to get stuck in the woods; but in the case of the social world, it's almost always possible to find a way to make a difference.

Before I say what those ways are, I need to offer two caveats. One is that the path to making a difference is not necessarily the path to happiness. Trying to change the world can entail conflict and strain. Even gentle challenges to the status quo can elicit criticism and hostility, and this is never pleasant. So if happiness is your first and foremost goal, then what I say is probably not going to be of much help. On the other hand, helping to create a better world can generate feelings of purpose and fulfillment, which might in turn lead to a more profound happiness. If you would like to consider how sociology can play a part in living such a life, please read on.

The second caveat is that even though the social world is always changing, this doesn't mean that our efforts to change it will produce quick and obvious results. It's important to keep this in mind, otherwise it's easy to get discouraged. Being sociologically mindful, we can think of our efforts to make a difference as contributions to an ongoing process, one that will outlast us by a long time. What matters, then, is how we choose to contribute to this process here and now. We can complain about problems but then act in a way that is likely to perpetuate them. Or we can go beyond complaining and try to act in a way that increases the chances that our lives will contribute to making the world a better place. Limited as our vision is, this is perhaps the best we can do.

I started this chapter with the question, *What does sociology say we should do about the problems that sociology makes visible?* The truth is, sociology doesn't say we should do anything to solve social problems. Sociology is an academic discipline, a body of ideas and information, a set of methods, a set of perspectives and theories for making sense of the social world. It doesn't say we should do any particular thing with whatever we find out about the social world. Only people, guided by moral principles that call for living an engaged life, can decide that the social conditions sociology brings to light are problems that demand solutions. This book is for those people.

The Book Ahead

The word "chapter" connotes something of significant length, as in a *chapter* in one's life. In books, too, chapters are often lengthy units of text that can be tiring to get through. I don't want that to be the case here. Yes, there are chapters, but short ones—shorter than the one you just read. It might be best to think of them as short essays rather than chapters. Each will deal with one practice that can be used in everyday life to make the world a better place.

Read the following chapters in sequence, if you wish. But there is no need to do so. Skipping around will work just as well; each essay can stand alone. In the last piece (chapter 12), I will say something about what I think all the chapters add up to. That will be, I hope, more than the sum of the parts—not just a set of practices but what some philosophers might call a *way*.

The full title of the book I mentioned earlier is *The Sociologically Examined Life: Pieces of the Conversation*. The subtitle was meant to convey the idea that I was not trying to have the last word but to add to a long conversation about sociology and how it can be used to understand social life. I see this book in the same way. It is not the last word but rather a contribution to a long conversation and to an ongoing process of social change. If it equips and inspires readers to participate in this conversation and carry it on, perhaps it will make a difference.

To Learn More

Berger, Peter. (1963). *Invitation to Sociology*. New York: Anchor Doubleday.

Callero, Peter. (2017). *The Myth of Individualism: How Social Forces Shape Our Lives* (3rd ed.). Lanham, MD: Rowman & Littlefield.

Korgen, Kathleen O., White, Jonathan M., and White, Shelley K. (2014). *Sociologists in Action: Sociology, Social Change, and Social Justice*. Thousand Oaks, CA: Sage.

Krause, Elliot. (1980). *Why Study Sociology?* New York: Random House.

Lee, Alfred McClung. (1978). *Sociology for Whom?* New York: Oxford University Press.

Mills, C. Wright. (1959). *The Sociological Imagination*. New York: Oxford University Press.

Nhat Hanh, Thich. (1975). *The Miracle of Mindfulness*. Boston: Beacon Press.

Nhat Hanh, Thich. (1992). *Peace Is Every Step: The Path of Mindfulness in Everyday Life*. New York: Bantam Books.

Schwalbe, Michael. (2015). *Rigging the Game: How Inequality Is Reproduced in Everyday Life* (2nd ed.). New York: Oxford University Press.

Schwalbe, Michael. (2018). *The Sociologically Examined Life: Pieces of the Conversation* (5th ed.). New York: Oxford University Press.

Sennett, Richard, and Cobb, Jonathan. (1972). *The Hidden Injuries of Class*. New York: Knopf.

Siegel, Ronald D. (2010). *The Mindfulness Solution*. New York: Guilford.

White, Shelley K., White, Jonathan, M., and Korgen, Kathleen, O. (2015). *Sociologists in Action on Inequalities: Race, Class, Gender, and Sexuality*. Thousand Oaks, CA: Sage.

CHAPTER 2

....

Listening

It seems like listening to others should be as natural and easy as breath-
ing. All we have to do is open our ears to what another person is saying,
and their message will come across clearly. Yet we know it's often not
so simple. Some messages can be hard to express. Some messages can be
hard to hear. And there is plenty that can interfere with listening.

Distraction is one obstacle to listening, especially in an era when
many people are riveted to their smartphones. Trying to multitask
when another person is talking is a way that we distract ourselves
from listening. Judgment can be another obstacle. If we are thinking
about what's wrong with what another person is saying—so that we
can object as soon as they're done speaking—then we are probably not
listening carefully.

It might seem strange, but fear can also be an obstacle to listening.
Sometimes we don't want to hear what another person is saying for
fear that it will hurt us in some way. Or we might be afraid that if we
listen closely, some belief that we cherish will be threatened. Not listening carefully then becomes a kind of defense against the possibility of
being upset or having to change our minds.

So what does listening have to do with making the world a better
place? It has quite a lot to do with it as it turns out. Consider what we
stand to lose by failing to listen carefully to others.

Most obviously, not listening means that we fail to learn. Others can be knowledgeable and have good information and ideas to offer. If we don't listen, or if our listening is impeded, we learn less than we could—and maybe some of what we miss is knowledge that would help us diagnose and solve problems. In short, by limiting what we learn, poor listening can diminish our power to make change.

Failing to listen can mean that we fail to understand how others see the world, the problems they face, and the suffering they experience. In this case, we might fail to appreciate that the world, or some part of it, needs changing because of the problems it causes. Part of making the world a better place is figuring out what's wrong with the status quo. This, too, is something we can learn by listening carefully.

By listening carefully, we often learn that others see and experience life differently from how we do. Being aware of this diversity of experience can improve our ability to communicate with a wide range of others. If we don't listen, we can end up with the false impression that everyone sees the world in the same way we do. Such an impression can create tensions that weaken collective efforts to make change. Listening is necessary to avoid or resolve those corrosive tensions.

Connecting with others by listening carefully is also part of how we build trust. When we listen and make others feel understood, they are more likely to trust us. Likewise, when others listen to us and we feel understood, we are more likely to trust them. Trust, in turn, is foundational to solidarity—that is, to being committed to working with others to pursue social change, especially when the going gets rough.

Listening matters even apart from efforts to change the world. We might know this from our own experience. When we feel isolated, anxious, depressed, or afraid, just being able to talk to someone who will listen carefully and nonjudgmentally can make us feel better. And of course, we can do the same for others. So even if we aren't engaged in a world-changing struggle, listening carefully can make a difference by reducing the amount of suffering in the world.

Failing to listen can also create suffering. Conflicts often persist because people are unwilling or unable to listen to each other carefully and thus fail to understand each other. This isn't to say that listening makes all conflicts disappear; that's clearly not the case. But we can't find workable compromises and figure out how to get along without listening. If making the world a better place means improving our abilities to negotiate peaceful solutions to conflicts, then listening is essential.

It seems true, then, that listening is an important part of social change; that failing to listen can cause problems; that there are obstacles to listening; and that overcoming these obstacles will improve our chances of making the world a better place. What all this suggests is that if we want to pursue change and make a difference in a positive way, it's necessary to learn to listen better. Here is where sociology can help.

How to Listen Mindfully

Sociologists who do interview studies and field research are professional listeners. We try to understand human behavior by asking questions to explore other people's experiences. This isn't as easy as it might sound. It takes practice to get good at asking the right question in the right way at the right time. But in addition to asking questions, we also have to get good at listening.

The kind of listening that interviewers and field researchers learn to do is sometimes called "active listening." As the term implies, this involves more than sitting back and letting another person's words wash over us. It involves making a conscious effort to engage with the other person. The specific things we can do, mentally and behaviorally, to listen more actively are described below.

Pay focused attention. This means giving the other person our full attention and ignoring distractions such as phones, computer screens, or things that are happening nearby. The goal of listening is to learn about the other person's experience, and anything that divides our attention interferes with achieving this goal. In a moment of distraction, we could miss a crucial piece of information, perhaps the piece that helps us make sense of the rest. Multitasking when trying to understand something as complex as another human being is a sure way to do a poor job of it.

Signal attention. We signal attention by maintaining eye contact, nodding our heads, and saying "uh huh" in response to what others say. These small behaviors tell others that we're tuned in and not drifting off. Others are likely to tell us more, more honestly, if we signal our attention in these ways. Signaling attention also helps us keep our attention focused, which in turn means that we will hear more.

Listen nonjudgmentally. If people think they are being judged for what they say, they will often censor themselves. If people feel they are being listened to and heard, not judged, they are more likely to speak openly and honestly. Even seemingly positive judgments—praising or cheering for something a person says—can have an inhibiting effect because every positive judgment ("Wow, that's cool!") implies that something else is less good, less worthy of being talked about. Good interviewers—those who are able to learn the most from other people—treat the other person with respect, while not conveying judgment about what s/he is saying.

Withhold advice. Researchers aren't usually tempted to give advice when they're doing interviews, since the goal is to gather data. In everyday life, however, the impulse to give advice can be strong. The problem is that when we give advice, we're not listening. Jumping in with advice might also make the other person feel incompetent, a feeling that probably won't incline them to keep talking. So it is generally better, if the goal is to understand a person by fully hearing them out, to withhold advice unless they ask for it.

Reflect and paraphrase. It can be hard to express complex thoughts and feelings. That's why people often say "Do you know what I mean?" after trying to describe an experience or explain an idea. As casual listeners, we might be quick to say yes, almost as a reflex response. But a more active listening technique is to paraphrase what we think the other person has said, then reflect it back to them for checking. This assures the other person that we're listening and trying to understand them. It also gives them a chance to clarify and add more information.

Ask questions. Researchers typically devote a great deal of care to crafting their questions in just the right way prior to an interview. But often the most effective questions are probes—follow-up questions formulated on the spot to elicit more information or clarify meanings. Active listening is not research, but it entails a kind of probing to make sure that we understand what the other person is saying. Sometimes a simple question—What do you mean by that?, or How did you feel about that?, or What happened then?—can be the invitation another person needs to open up to us.

Listen for the whole message. Sometimes people say one thing on the surface ("I like school") and something else beneath the surface ("I like school, but there are parts I dislike, so I'm really kind of ambivalent about it"). Active listening means listening for the subtext, the message beneath the surface. This means paying attention not only to what is said but how it's said. Again, it's important to reflect and paraphrase to make sure that we've got the message right and that we aren't imagining a subtext that isn't really there.

Stay in the moment. It's easy for our minds to drift off when we talk with others. We might start thinking about what we're going to do later in the day. Or we might be thinking about what we're going to say when it's our turn to talk. When this happens, we're no longer truly listening. The active listening techniques just described will help overcome this problem. It also helps to be aware of the tendency and to resist it. When we notice our minds wandering, we can bring our focus back to the present moment and the person who is right in front of us.

These techniques of active listening aren't intended to turn everyday conversations into research interviews. Rather, these are techniques that researchers use to do a better job of something that is no less important in everyday life: understanding others and their experiences. As I suggested earlier, understanding others is part of learning from them, building trust, and maintaining solidarity—all of which can inspire and bolster efforts to create social change. So, as simple as it sounds, listening is a practice at which we can get better and in the process gain power to make a difference.

When I teach interviewing techniques, I tell students that it doesn't take hundreds of research interviews to refine their skills. I say that interviewing skills can be practiced whenever we have a serious conversation with another person. The same point applies to the advice I've offered here. For most of us, everyday life provides opportunities to practice active listening. And, like anything else, the more we practice, the better we get. In the case of active listening, the better we get, the more we learn and the more deeply we connect with others who might also want to make the world a better place.

Listening Beyond Hearing

The way I have described listening so far conjures an image of two people in close conversation. This is indeed the image I wanted to conjure; active listening is mainly about what we do in one-on-one conversations. But listening can also be thought of more broadly, as a kind of seeking and tuning in to divergent perspectives that are present in the social world. Think of a satellite dish that sweeps the sky for signals that can be decoded to obtain potentially useful information. We can try to be like this, figuratively speaking.

Listening, I am suggesting, can be more than paying close attention to people with whom we routinely cross paths. We might go beyond this and seek to cross paths with others who have something useful or important to tell us about the social world—something we don't already know. This can be an even harder kind of listening to practice because it means going out of our way to hear things we might not want to hear. Here is an example.

A few years ago, a white student in my social inequality course said to me, after class, that he disliked the slogan "black lives matter" because he thought all lives should matter. I said that he should explore the meaning of "black lives matter" more deeply and that he might start by asking one of his black friends to explain it to him. He responded with silence, which I took to mean that he didn't have any black friends to ask. So I suggested that he ask another student in class, a black woman who struck me as being smart and politically savvy. To my surprise, he did this, and later he made a comment in class to the effect that the slogan "black lives matter" did not mean that *only* black lives matter but that black lives matter, *too*. He had listened.

The nudge I gave my student is one that we can learn to give ourselves. When we become aware of views that baffle or irritate us, we can go out of our way to listen to those who express those views and try to understand them (see chapter 6 on empathizing). This doesn't mean that we accept those views—we might still think they're wrong. What it means is that we will have a better idea of precisely what those views are, where they come from, and how they make sense to the people who embrace them.

Sociologists do this sort of thing all the time. Many research projects grow out of curiosity about how the conditions of people's lives lead them to see the world in particular ways. Listening is an essential part of the process. One thing we usually learn, after listening carefully and considering the conditions of people's lives, is that how they see the world actually does make sense (though, again, this doesn't mean taking what they say as true). By listening carefully in everyday life—and going out of our way to listen to more voices—we might arrive at a similar insight: that even those whose views seem strange or wrong can teach us something about the social world, if only how it looks from one corner.

Just as we can listen more or less well when people talk to us, we can listen more or less well when people write. "Listening," in other words, can be taken to include listening to texts—the articles and books we read, whether in print or online. This is another form of listening that works better when it is active rather than passive.

In college, most of us learn to listen to texts in a critical way. We learn to play what Peter Elbow, an English professor and writing teacher, calls the doubting game. By this he means that we learn to look for what's wrong with what we're reading so that we can avoid being fooled by a specious argument, or so that we can show how smart we are. Of course, there is nothing wrong with being skeptical. But Elbow says that when we play the doubting game, we risk not fully grasping what we're reading because we're too busy looking for what's wrong to see what's right and useful. It's a kind of bad listening.

The other way to approach a piece of writing, Elbow says, is by playing the believing game. In this case, instead of trying to find what's wrong with what a writer says, we try to believe it. To do this, Elbow recommends that we try to see through the eyes of the writer to figure out why the writer believes what she or he is saying is true. This can help us understand more of what a writer is saying. Playing the believing game also helps us find what is useful in a piece of writing—something that we might overlook if we are intent only on finding what's wrong or something with which to disagree. Playing the believing game, I would say, is a better way to listen to a text.

The advice to play the believing game makes some people anxious. What if, in playing the believing game, we end up being seduced by a writer peddling bad ideas or information? What if, by trying to believe what a writer says, we end up overlooking weak arguments and inadequate evidence? And doesn't playing the believing game compromise one's independence of mind? These are fair questions. But if we play the believing game as a conscious strategy, we needn't worry about being fooled. Playing the believing game doesn't mean giving up one's independence of mind. It means using that independence differently. In the end, it remains up to us to decide what to believe. In fact, by reading or listening more closely, we might see more clearly where an argument goes wrong as well as what might be reasonable about it. This represents a potentially valuable intellectual gain, relative to listening or reading in a less attentive way. What we gain, along with a deeper understanding of others, is a greater ability to make intelligent, well-informed judgments of our own.

A final point: getting the most out of the techniques I've described here doesn't come just from *appearing* to be a better listener or reader. It comes from taking in and reflecting on what we hear and read. Playing the believing game is a step in this direction. We also need to think about how what we've taken in, by way of new information about others' thoughts and feelings, makes sense in light of the conditions of their lives and their experiences. This kind of deeper, sustained reflection is what turns active listening into sociologically mindful listening, which is what can turn information into understanding.

To Learn More

Forsey, Martin G. (2010). "Ethnography as Participant Listening." *Ethnography* 11(4): 558–572.

Nichols, Michael P. (2009). *The Lost Art of Listening* (2nd ed.). New York: Guilford.

Rebach, Howard M. (2001). "Communication and Relationships with Clients." Pp. 37–51 in H. M. Rebach and J. G. Bruhn (eds.), *Handbook of Clinical Sociology*. New York: Kluwer Academic/Plenum Publishers.

Rogers, Carl, and Farson, Richard. (1979). "Active Listening." Pp. 168–180 in D. A. Kolb, I. M. Rubin, and J. M. McIntyre (eds.), *Organizational Psychology* (3rd ed.). Englewood Cliffs, New Jersey: Prentice-Hall.

Rosenberg, Marshall B. (2015). *Nonviolent Communication: A Language of Life* (3rd ed.). Del Mar, CA: Puddledancer Press.

Shafir, Rebecca Z. (2003). *The Zen of Listening*. Wheaton, IL: Quest Books.

Weiss, Robert S. (1995). *Learning from Strangers: The Art and Method of Qualitative Interview Studies*. New York: The Free Press.

CHAPTER 3

Researching

Imagine that you are experiencing swollen lymph nodes in your neck, a persistent fever, joint pain, headaches, dizziness, a rash, fatigue, and nausea. You're worried, so you see a doctor. You describe your symptoms, and the doctor says, "Wow, that's weird. I have no idea what's wrong with you. Take it easy for a few weeks and call me if you're not feeling better. Good luck." You would probably be unsatisfied with such a response.

The doctor in this example doesn't know enough to make a diagnosis. To be more helpful, s/he needs to examine you more closely, run some tests, and perhaps consult a medical database or other doctors. This is a lot like what any of us might do when we face a baffling problem. We look at it more closely, we look for what is already known about it or similar problems, we look for more knowledgeable others who can help us make sense of what we're seeing. All this looking can also be called researching.

We usually think of research as the work of highly educated specialists. Perhaps we imagine white-coated chemists in a laboratory full of beakers, test tubes, and microscopes; or archaeologists in shorts, T-shirts, and sandals using trowels to scrounge for bones in the dirt; or historians scrutinizing musty tomes. But if we broaden our conception of research to include all searching for truthful knowledge and information that is new to us, then it begins to look a lot more like what many people do, or could do, in everyday life.

It might help to distinguish between several types of research. One type is routine these days: looking up answers to specific questions, either online or in print. A second type is more formal and usually done for a special purpose; for example, gathering facts for a writing project (see chapter 4) or an organizing effort (see chapter 5). A third type of research is scholarly or scientific. This is even more rigorous and usually aims to discover new facts, not just look up what is already known.

What do these types of research have to do with making the world a better place? The short answer is that research is how we obtain the information needed to analyze problems and talk constructively about possible solutions. In the face of a problem we would like to solve but don't fully understand, research is how we find a way forward. We search again (and again, if necessary) for the facts we need, or for theories to explain the facts we have, so that we can get a better grip on what's happening and what needs to be done.

To say that research helps us solve problems might seem banal. If our car won't start, if we have strange bodily pains, if a computer program doesn't work right—if we are stumped by any kind of problem—we need to "do research" in the form of seeking helpful information. Likewise, if we want to find a cure for cancer or new forms of clean energy, it's clear that scientific research will be needed. All this is obvious. But here's the hitch: despite the high values placed on science and research in our society, in everyday life we often do a poor job of finding out what we need to know to participate in analyzing and solving social problems. I'm going to suggest how we can do better.

In writing about teaching (see chapter 9), I say that everybody can live as a teacher even if they don't make a living as a teacher. All that's necessary is being more mindful of how we teach by example and of how we can help others gain knowledge and skill. The same principle applies to researching. Although the world would probably be a better place if more people chose careers in research, this isn't practical for everyone. But what everyone can do is to appreciate the values that underlie good research and try to put those values into practice when "looking stuff up," when trying to analyze the social world, and when talking about possible solutions to social problems. All this is doable without being a full-time scientist or scholar.

Some readers probably will agree about the value of scientific or scholarly research, but they think that in everyday life, "researching" is unnecessary. After all, quick and dirty answers are often good enough. Experts can be found if more knowledge is called for. And, what's more, why bother? The experts and power brokers will do what they want anyway, regardless of what ordinary people know or don't know. All these things might be true, much of the time. But accepting them means accepting the status quo, and that's not what this book is about.

If we want to participate in solving social problems, not just sit on the sidelines, we need to be mindful of the value of research, be able to evaluate it, and be able to use good research practices in our own fact-finding. If we can do these things, we are more likely to be heard, less likely to be misled by bad analysis, better able to listen, and better able to talk about possible solutions. In short, researching—in the broad sense I mean here—is a practice that enhances our ability to help make the world a better place. Again, this is possible without getting a PhD. Here is how.

The Background Rules of Research

If you want to learn how to do surveys, interviews, or experiments, you will have to look elsewhere. I'm not going to describe research methods at that level of detail. Rather, I want to highlight the background rules of research. These are the sometimes unspoken rules that guide research in scholarly and scientific fields, though they aren't only for scholars and scientists. Anyone who wants to seriously investigate the social world can do a better job of it by following these rules. And the better our inquiries, even as citizen investigators, the better able we will be to participate in solving social problems.

Ask answerable questions. As researchers, we don't want to try tackling unanswerable questions. But some questions are more yielding than others. Suppose we asked, what causes success or failure in school? Although this is an answerable question, it's huge; it would take a great deal of time and effort to answer it. So it might be better to ask a question that focuses more narrowly on what is of most interest to us. We might ask, for example, does family income affect success in school, all else being equal? It would still take some work to come up with a good answer, but it wouldn't be a life's work. A useful rule, then, is to get our questions down to manageable proportions so that we are not trying to explain the entire universe at once.

Define key terms. If we were going to study success in school, we would have to decide what we mean by success: Do we mean grades? Do we mean graduating on time? Do we mean test scores? And what kind of schools are we talking about? We would need to define these terms—and identify indicators or measures of what the terms refer to—before we could proceed. All researchers must do a similar thing; only by precisely defining key terms can they understand and evaluate each other's methods and findings. In everyday life, we often fail to define our terms carefully enough, leading us to talk past each other when we talk about social problems. We can do better than this if we do what researchers do: nail down, and try to agree on, the meaning of key terms.

Start with what's already known. An old research maxim says that a year of primary data collection can save a few hours in the library. This is a joke because the opposite is supposed to happen; research is supposed to start with the library (or the online equivalent) so that time isn't wasted trying to rediscover what's already known. So, for example, if we wanted to know whether family income affects success in school, the first thing to do would be to look for studies that address this question. A good answer might already exist. Most researchers begin a project in this way—by "reviewing the literature." It's not easy for everyone to access and assess the scholarly literature on a topic, yet this is a crucial first step. If more people did this, there would be fewer arguments about matters that are already settled.

Ask for help in finding out what's known. Researchers at the cutting edge of their fields rarely need help of this kind, but students and beginners do. It might not be obvious where to look or which literature to review. People who are already expert in a field can provide direction. So can good research librarians (who usually work in university libraries). Busy experts can't respond to every request for help, but librarians are often eager to do so. The world would be a better place, I've often thought, if more people took advantage of librarians' skills in finding reliable information about all manner of things. The information we need—and perhaps more than we imagined existed—is often ours for the taking if we can just get a little help in tracking it down.

Evaluate what's known. Answers to our questions might already exist, but are they correct? The only way to decide is to evaluate the quantity and quality of the evidence. Suppose we find 90 studies showing that family income affects success in school, and 10 that show otherwise. In this case, the weight of the evidence is on the side of family income having an effect. But we would also need to look at the quality of the studies. Perhaps the studies showing no effect are weak or flawed, while the ones showing an effect are well done. If so, then both the quantity and quality of the evidence are on the side of income having an effect. Part of being trained to do research in a field is learning how to assess studies in these ways. If you don't (yet) have this training, ask for help.

Evaluating what's known includes considering the source of knowledge. Researchers who have no stake in an issue are probably more trustworthy than analysts employed by outfits that exist to promote a political or economic agenda. Studies published in peer-reviewed journals are likely to be more reliable than reports presented directly to the public. Information or analysis should not be judged based solely on its source, yet it's wise to take the possible biases of a source into account when evaluating knowledge claims. Here again it might be good to seek expert advice in making this kind of determination.

Look for counterevidence and alternative explanations. Research should lead to answers that are dictated by evidence, not politics. But this can happen only if we look at and evaluate all the evidence, not just the evidence we like. Suppose, for example, that someone wanted to deny that family income affects success in school. They might find a few studies showing that income doesn't matter—and tout these as proof that it doesn't matter—while ignoring the more numerous and stronger studies showing that it does. This is called "cherry-picking" and is a mistake often made by people who are untrained as scholars or scientists. But whether we are scientists, scholars, or citizen investigators, getting at the truth of a matter requires looking at all the evidence. Because we tend to see what we want to see, it's necessary to make a point of looking for evidence that challenges what we would like to believe is true. We must still assess the evidence and decide what's credible, but we can't assess what we overlook.

It might seem that if we can just find trustworthy facts and add them up correctly, we will have the answer to whatever question prompted our research. Well, perhaps this is so. But facts always need to be interpreted, and there might be more than one way to explain the facts we've gathered. If a new theory more neatly accounts for more of the facts than the theory we began with, then we should revise our thinking accordingly. This would be a good outcome because it means we've found a better way to understand what's going on. We are more likely to arrive at this result if our research process includes considering both counterevidence and alternative explanations of all the credible evidence we've been able to gather.

Be skeptical, not cynical. In the face of counterevidence and competing theories, it's easy to despair of ever finding the right answer to a question. It's then tempting to stop trying to find right answers and decide to believe whatever feels right or is most comforting. This is what happens when skepticism slides into cynicism—a stance that treats all knowledge claims as corrupted by bias and thus equally unreliable. This stance goes too far. Researchers know that even the best answers produced by the best methods of inquiry are bound to be incomplete and uncertain—as is always the case with human knowledge. If we are willing to accept this uncertainty, and yet make serious efforts to seek the best answers we can find, we will learn more, know more, and act more effectively than if we stop trying to distinguish better answers from worse ones.

Consider degrees of confidence. In everyday life, we tend to think of most knowledge claims as either true or false. With some claims—for example, "I was born within the last 200 years"—it makes sense to treat them this way. But as knowledge claims become more nuanced, and as they require more complex inquiry to verify, it is better to think in terms of degrees of confidence. This is especially important when we make claims about the social world.

Suppose, for example, we did the appropriate research and then made this claim: the higher a family's income, up to twice the national household median, the more successful its children will be in school, all else being equal. That claim implies a complex reality requiring a complex research process to sort out. The research behind the claim might also be stronger in some ways than in others. We might have excellent data about some things (e.g., student success, family income) and poor data about others (e.g., teachers' expectations, classroom environments). So we might be more sure about having gotten some things right than about others that are harder to measure.

Most research-based claims about the social world are like this. The research behind the claims might be sound, but because there are complex processes operating that are hard to tease out, we qualify our claims. Instead of saying X is true, we say that, based on the strengths and weaknesses of the methods used to determine whether X is true, we are __% confident that it is. This is how social researchers avoid overstating their certainty. If we did this more often when talking about social problems, we might be less likely to end up in fruitless arguments because people insist on the absolute truth or falsity of knowledge claims, without thinking carefully about how much confidence those claims warrant, given how they were arrived at.

Be systematic. Research often uncovers patterns that are not visible to the casual observer. For example, someone might say, "I've seen kids from poor families who get straight As, so it's clear that family income doesn't matter for success in school." The first part of the statement might be true as a report of personal experience, but it's based on limited, haphazard observation, so it can't validly support any generalizations. To find out whether family income matters, it's necessary to observe systematically—to gather all the relevant information, in a consistent way, over time, from many cases, and then analyze the information using methods that control for bias. We aren't likely to do all this when questions arise in everyday life. But if we can appreciate the necessity of doing it, we can put more trust in claims that result from doing it, and we can try—see the chapters on empathizing and teaching—to explain these principles to others.

Examine assumptions. All research is built on some set of assumptions, some set of ideas about what can be taken for granted. Assumptions (also called premises or axioms) are necessary because it's impossible, when doing research, to put everything into question at once; some things simply must be taken for granted or else we couldn't proceed at all. The problem is that if we've assumed something that isn't true, we can end up reaching false conclusions. Which is why it's a good idea to do what good researchers occasionally do: examine our assumptions.

Suppose that in studying success in school we looked only at what happens in school. We might look at class size, teaching methods, the types of classes offered, and so on. We might also look at student behavior. In the end, we might conclude that teacher behavior is the best predictor of student success. But this could be misleading because we've assumed that what happens outside of school doesn't matter. Perhaps if we also looked at family income, parents' education, and parents' involvement in school activities, we would find that these variables are far better predictors of success. In this case, a wrong assumption would have led us to a wrong conclusion. The only way to avoid this kind of problem is to reflect on what we are taking for granted as true—what we are not putting into question—and on how this might affect what we can find out. We can do the same thing in everyday life. We can pause to think about what we are assuming to be true, perhaps without adequate basis for belief.

Following the background rules that I've just sketched is what lends credibility to research. If we gather information without following these rules, the results are likely to be dismissed as unreliable. By knowing and following the rules (and other proper methods for gathering and analyzing data), it is possible for anyone to produce credible, trustworthy results. Knowing these rules of inquiry is thus an important kind of knowledge in itself. What we thereby gain is the ability to understand the world more accurately and fully. As I suggest in the next section, this ability in turn gives us more power as citizens who have a stake in solving social problems.

Knowledge and Power

One assumption I've made here is that more knowledge—found or created through sound research—is better than less knowledge. I say "better" because knowledge is what allows us to act effectively; it gives us the power to solve problems. So, by definition, if unsolved problems keep the world from being as good a place as it might be, and if research helps us solve these problems, then researching is one way to make the world a better place. At least this is true in general. In real life, things are more complicated.

For one thing, the kind of knowledge being sought matters. Research that seeks knowledge useful for building more destructive weapons will not make the world a better place. Research that seeks knowledge useful for manufacturing harmful products will not make the world a better place, nor will research that gives political and economic elites more power to control everyone else. So when I say that research can make the world a better place, I mean research that helps reduce suffering, violence, exploitation, and injustice.

Research must also be put to use. Knowledge left to rest in texts doesn't do much good. Somehow this knowledge needs to be found and used to guide action aimed at constructive social change. This is why I advised, as part of being a "citizen investigator," researching in the form of finding out what is already known. Such knowledge can then be put to use in organizing, teaching, advocating, and writing. If it leads people to more effectively resist domination and exploitation, then it can make a positive difference.

Political and economic elites understand that knowledge bolsters their power. This might be scientific knowledge of some kind, it might be knowledge of laws and policies, it might be knowledge of how the economy or government operates, or it might be knowledge about how people can be enticed to buy things they don't need. When knowledge about these matters is unequally distributed, democracy suffers because some people are better able to pursue their interests than others. Researching, especially truth seeking by ordinary people, can help to offset these imbalances.

This brings us back to a problem I noted earlier: if people feel powerless to make a difference no matter how much they learn, they probably won't put much effort into researching. This is a real problem. It can seem pointless to seek knowledge about how society works if it seems that there is no way to put that knowledge to use. Another way to look at it, however, is that gaining knowledge is a necessary step toward gaining a fair share of power in a democratic society. Rather than let feelings of powerlessness deter us from seeking knowledge, we might seek knowledge as way to overcome those paralyzing feelings.

Change requires more, of course, than just knowing things. We must also use what we know to guide action. This could be individual action, such as voting in a more informed way or writing more persuasively. Or it could be collective action, such as organizing to challenge abusive authority or get a candidate elected to office. When the knowledge gained through researching changes how we do things together—when it enables us to act more effectively together—it can do the most to make the world a better place.

In chapter 4 on writing (coming up next), I advise seeking guidance from more experienced writers. I advise the same thing when it comes to researching. The best way to learn background rules and methods of procedure is not from textbooks but from working alongside well-trained, experienced researchers. My final suggestion, then, is to seek opportunities to get involved in doing some kind of research. Whether or not you want to do research for a living, what you learn is likely to enhance your power to live in a way that makes a difference.

To Learn More

Babbie, Earl R. (2015). *The Practice of Social Research* (14th ed.). Belmont, CA: Wadsworth.

Becker, Howard S. (1998). *Tricks of the Trade: How to Think About Your Research While You're Doing It*. Chicago: University of Chicago Press.

Bloomfield, Victor A., and El-Fakahany, E. (2008). *The Chicago Guide to Your Career in Science*. Chicago: University of Chicago Press.

Booth, Wayne C., Colomb, Gregory G., Williams, Joseph M., Bizup, Joseph, and Fitzgerald, William T. (2016). *The Craft of Research* (4th ed.). Chicago: University of Chicago Press.

Kleinman, Sherryl. (2007). *Feminist Fieldwork Analysis*. Thousand Oaks, CA: Sage.

Kuhn, Thomas. ([1962] 2012). *The Structure of Scientific Revolutions* (50th anniversary ed.). Chicago: University of Chicago Press.

Levitin, Daniel J. (2016). *Weaponized Lies: How to Think Critically in the Post-Truth Era*. New York: Dutton.

Oreskes, Naomi, and Conway, Erik M. (2010). *Merchants of Doubt: How a Handful of Scientists Obscured the Truth on Issues from Tobacco Smoke to Global Warming*. New York: Bloomsbury Press.

Ostergard, Robert L., and Fisher, Stacy B. (2017). *Kickstarting Your Academic Career: Skills to Succeed in the Social Sciences*. Toronto, ON: University of Toronto Press.

Schick, Theodore, and Vaughn, Lewis. (2013). *How to Think About Weird Things: Critical Thinking for a New Age* (7th ed.). New York: McGraw-Hill.

Swedberg, Richard. (2014). *The Art of Social Theory*. Princeton, NJ: Princeton University Press.

CHAPTER 4

....

Writing

I once had a graduate student who was a terrible writer. Her sentences were awkward and murky. Her paragraphs were jumbles of thoughts that didn't hang together to make a point. Reading her papers was exhausting because of the effort required to figure out what she was trying to say. She knew that she needed to become a better writer, so she took my writing course.

One day in class I had students do a free-writing exercise. The instructions were to write for ten minutes—without pausing, without revising, without worrying about what anyone else would think—starting with the prompt, "What I'd really like to study is. . . ." I then had everyone read their pages aloud. The student who was a bad writer wrote about studying women's sports. Her free write was clear, smooth, smart, and full of energy. I was amazed.

Later I said to her that I thought she ought to stop studying crime and study women's sports. It seemed clear that was what she cared about, and that caring made her writing sing. "I can't do that," she said, indicating that she was going to stick to crime. When I asked why, she said, "If I study women's sports, nobody will take me seriously." She was being overly pessimistic, but she wasn't entirely wrong; in academia, some topics are taken more seriously than others.

Unfortunately, this student was not unusual. Many students suffer from the same problem. They write badly not because they can't do better but because they are compelled to write about things that don't matter to them. Writing is done as a performance for the teacher—a song and dance for the sake of a grade. These conditions seldom elicit a person's best work. Even worse, these conditions tend to make people hate writing. The good news is that writing to make a difference is not like writing in school. For one thing, it's not done for a grade. It's done to influence others by sharing a meaningful experience or by making an argument. Another difference is that the motivation comes from inside because the writer feels strongly that there is something—a problem, a state of affairs, an idea—that others need to be made aware of. Under these conditions, when people are writing from the heart, writing is not the onerous, pointless practice that it can feel like in school.

Many people who struggle to write well in school might come to think they are bad writers and thus shy away from public writing. They might think that they lack the talent to write in a way powerful enough to affect others. But as the case of my graduate student suggests, the problem is not a lack of talent but a lack of caring and purpose. In fact, I would say that, under the right conditions, anyone who can write at all is capable of doing the kind of public writing that can make a difference in the world.

What I mean by "public writing" is writing intended to reach readers who might be complete strangers. This is one thing that makes public writing different from sending e-mails or text messages to friends. Public writing also typically concerns some matter that has implications for the lives of the unknown others whom a writer is trying to reach. If you e-mail a friend about a new video game you've just purchased, that is private writing. If you review the game for a website, perhaps advising readers to shun the game because of its violent imagery, that is public writing.

Other examples of public writing are letters to the editor of a newspaper, op-eds or guest columns (again, usually in newspapers), comments in online forums, blogs, articles for print magazines or websites, and books. This kind of writing can reach thousands, sometimes millions of people and affect how they think, feel, and behave. It certainly has the potential to make a difference—even to make the world a better place, depending on how it's done. Sociology can help with this.

Most people who want to write for a wide audience probably don't think of sociology as a place to turn for advice. The truth is, sociologists have a reputation for being lousy writers. We are often accused of using pretentious jargon to say things that could be better said in plain English. It's also true that a lot of sociology in academic journals is dull and hard to read. Sociology doesn't have to be written this way, but I can't deny that much of it is. So I am sympathetic to readers who are skeptical about sociology helping anyone do a better job of public writing.

But my claim isn't that academic writing by sociologists is a model for public writing (although some of it is a model of what not to do). My claim, rather, is that public writing can be more effective if it is done in a sociologically mindful way. This is something that anyone who wants to write about social issues, especially contentious ones, can learn to do. I am also hoping that by showing how to take a sociologically mindful approach to public writing, more people will want to do it as another way of trying to make the world a better place.

How to Write to and for Others

Advice about how to write is abundant. There are hundreds of books and thousands of articles offering tips and suggestions. Much of the advice is excellent. *Avoid clichés. Eliminate clutter. Use active verbs. Prefer shorter words to longer ones.* I agree that these are good things to do (I try to do them myself). But the kind of advice I have to offer is different. It's less about how to write good sentences than it is about how to write something of value to others.

Good sentences are important, of course. Clarity and apt expression— using the right words in the right order, with originality and style— are what grip readers and get a message across. But putting too much stress on artfulness can make public writing seem daunting. "I'm not a good enough writer," many people might think. Seeing public writing as mere self-expression is another problem because then people equate it with being a show-off or a loudmouth.

My suggestion is to think of public writing as joining a conversation. This doesn't require literary mastery, just some care and a bit of craft. And it isn't about showing off. It's about entering into a relationship with one's neighbors or fellow citizens for the sake of addressing matters of mutual concern—like talking over a backyard fence or a café table, only with many people at once. Here, then, are seven suggestions for how to do this in a sociologically mindful way.

Respect readers. It's hard to get others to join us in conversation if we start by saying something insulting or condescending. If that's how others perceive us, they probably won't stick around to hear what we have to say. The same is true for writing. As writers, we want readers to attend to our words. But if the words convey an attitude of contempt, readers will turn away. This is especially true in the case of public writing, when we are trying to reach readers who aren't obligated by bonds of friendship to pay attention.

Respecting the reader means taking the reader seriously as an intelligent partner in conversation. It means addressing the reader as someone whose attention we earn by being clear, informative, and sensitive to differences of perspective and opinion. Imagine a kind of golden rule applied to writing. The way we would like to be addressed as readers—with respect for our time, intelligence, and humanity—is the way we, as public writers, should try to address readers. This doesn't guarantee that readers will stick around, but it increases the odds; and getting readers to keep reading is a prerequisite for getting a message across.

Respect opponents. Public writing is often driven by strong feelings about social or political issues. These feelings make it tempting to use snarky language to refer to people who hold contrary views. I understand the impulse to do so. I know how satisfying it can feel to write a witty barb that skewers one's opponents. The problem is that conveying disrespect for opponents is often counterproductive. For one thing, it gives opponents a reason to turn away. Who wants to endure a barrage of insults?

Perhaps few people who are committed to views contrary to ours will read or take seriously what we say in any case. Still, they might, and this is a possibility worth keeping in mind. But there might be many other readers who are, as pollsters say, "undecided." These readers are open to persuasion, or at least to considering a new point of view. It is these readers who can be put off by rudeness and disrespect aimed at some group of people, even if this occurs in the context of an otherwise sound argument.

Respecting opponents doesn't mean giving credence to views that are illogical, irrational, or inhumane—as if all sides of an issue are of equal value for creating a better world. What it means, rather, is respecting the humanity of those who hold opposing views, even if we think those views are egregiously, even dangerously, wrong. This doesn't imply less vigor in opposing illogical, irrational, or inhumane views, just wariness against the tendency to dehumanize others. By avoiding this tendency in public writing, it's possible to engage and persuade more readers while also modeling part of what a better world would look like.

Anticipate objections. Making an argument implies that there is a viewpoint against which an argument needs to be made. People who take this other view are naturally going to have objections and criticisms. Even people who don't take an opposing view might have objections or criticisms if an argument strikes them as weak. A good strategy, then, is to anticipate what opponents, critics, and skeptics might say in response to a piece of public writing—and then deal with those responses in the piece itself.

Anticipating objections takes effort. It requires figuring out what the objections are likely to be. It also requires handling those objections fairly and not in a caricatured (or "strawperson") way. Sometimes this is hard to do because opposing views can seem terribly wrong. But if we don't take these views into account and deal with them seriously, we weaken our writing. Critics and skeptics can say that we got it wrong because we ignored key facts or alternative interpretations. Taking these facts and interpretations into account still might not sway dedicated opponents, but it does make an argument harder to dismiss. It also makes the argument more persuasive to those who have not yet staked out a position.

We can't count on others to play the believing game (see chapter 2) when they read what we write. Some will—especially when we are preaching to the choir, as the saying goes. But many are likely to play the doubting game, looking for reasons to reject what we say. If we acknowledge possible objections, take those objections seriously, and respond to them preemptively, then what we write will be more persuasive to more readers. By anticipating objections, we also complicate and refine our views and perhaps discover what we have in common with others—the things about which we agree and can build on in searching for solutions to social problems.

Gather facts. Public writing often makes claims about what is true. Before making such claims, we should try to be as sure of our facts as possible. A prior step is to think about readers. We might ask ourselves, what facts would a reader need to judge the truth of what we're saying? If we can answer this question, we can then gather the facts needed to give a piece of writing some persuasive heft.

But how do we know that the facts we find are correct? How do we know when we have enough facts? It would take a long digression to fully answer these questions. Here are two short answers.

First, we should be wary of facts that come from people or organizations that are driven by a political or economic agenda. For example, a source that is funded by wealthy industrialists who want to eliminate government regulation, lower corporate taxes, and rely on the market to solve every problem is probably not a trustworthy source of unbiased facts. It would be better to seek more neutral or objective sources.

Second, if we don't have enough facts to complicate our thinking— to make us pause and wonder if we're right—then we probably need to keep digging. A good idea is to look for facts that don't neatly support what we already think is true and wrestle with those facts. This kind of fact gathering is what makes the difference between a rant and a solid argument that musters evidence and respects the complexity of the real world. As a piece of public writing, the latter is likely to be more effective.

Another way to think of fact gathering is as a form of service to readers, not just as a means to persuade. If we focus solely on persuasion, we will be tempted to seek and present only those facts that support our case while ignoring others. But if we think of public writing as a form of education, then we will seek and present facts that help readers better understand what's going on. When public writing is done this way—with respect for reliable facts, for complexity, and for readers—it can make us all a little smarter as social analysts.

Connect stories to data. Sometimes a piece of public writing is basically a story—a writer describes his or her experience, or someone else's experience, and offers it to readers as a form of evidence, like giving testimony in court. A writer might then go on to draw out the lesson of the story, or leave it to readers to find the lesson. Either way, this kind of public writing works because of the power of stories to captivate us and make issues come to life in our minds. But here is the problem with stories: as powerful as they can be, they can also be dismissed as mere stories—stuff somebody just made up.

A way to overcome this problem, while also exploiting the power of stories, is to connect stories to data. For example, suppose someone wanted to show how rising tuition costs have made it harder for people from working-class families to attend college. A person could do this by telling his or her personal story of struggling to earn and borrow enough money to pay tuition bills. It would be even better, however, if the personal story was shown to be representative of many other people. Citing reliable statistics about working-class wage stagnation, rising tuition costs (even after controlling for inflation), and increasing student debt would help to show that the story is not idiosyncratic but that it potentially mirrors the experience of millions of students.

Every personal story can be contextualized by connecting it to data about larger social or economic trends and conditions. When a story is connected to data in this way, it becomes harder for critics to dismiss it as a mere story or the story of one disgruntled person. Another way to think of this is as using personal stories to illustrate patterns that can be verified with data. This is a powerful strategy for public writing, as it can affect not only people's thoughts about social problems but also the feelings that move them to try to make a difference.

Get feedback. Strong feelings about an issue can lead to writing that is authentic and lively. Yet passion can sometimes make us forget that our writing must be clear to others. We can get so caught up in the act of expression—trying to put our feelings into words—that we fail in the act of communication—getting across information, ideas, and an argument. Respecting readers, respecting opponents, and anticipating objections help to minimize this problem. It also helps to get feedback on writing that we want to make public.

Getting feedback means sharing what we write with a friend or colleague before making it public. The friend or colleague serves as a test reader: someone who will tell us if our writing "works" or not. Maybe a sentence is unclear, or an argument is weak, or we've misused a word. Or maybe we've unwittingly said something that will offend the people we're trying to reach. A good test reader will spot these problems and help fix them. I suggest getting feedback from more than one test reader because different readers will often spot different problems.

Sociologists and other academic folks do this sort of thing all the time. Every published book and article has been revised multiple times based on prepublication feedback. I don't mean that every tweet or blog post has to go through this kind of process (though it would probably keep some people from saying foolish things in haste). But the more important a piece of public writing is—the more important it is that the writing produce its intended effect—the more worthwhile it is to get feedback ahead of time. Getting feedback from experienced writers is also how one becomes a better writer in the long run.

Be cooperative. If you publish your own blog, you're the boss. You can write pretty much whatever you want at whatever length you want, and no editor will reject your submission. But suppose you want to reach a different audience, perhaps by publishing a letter or an op-ed (guest column) in a newspaper, an essay on a website, or an article in a magazine. If you want to do this kind of public writing, you'll need to be mindful of someone else's rules.

These rules are not secret. Most print and online publications have guidelines for submission that specify length for letters, columns, essays, and other kinds of articles. If letters are limited to 250 words, don't send a 500-word letter and expect it to get published. If guest columns are limited to 750 words, don't send in a 1500-word piece. If essays are supposed to be written in a clear, accessible style, don't send an academic paper full of jargon. When in doubt, ask. Or try googling first.

Mainstream publications get more submissions than they can publish. So an easy way to eliminate the excess is to reject everything that doesn't follow the rules. This isn't to say that there is never any flexibility; editors can decide, if there is a good reason, to allow a little wiggle room on length limits. But don't count on it. The best chance of having your work—some piece of public writing—accepted for publication comes from offering strong content (see the previous bits of advice) and following the rules set by editorial gatekeepers.

Here is one more bit of advice related to following the rules: read like a writer. Look at the place in which you'd like to publish and pick out the pieces of writing that strike you as well done. Then study *how* they're done. Look at how they're organized and the style in which they're written. The idea is not to mimic someone else's writing, but to find a model to guide your own efforts. Looking for good models and striving to meet high standards involves more work than sending a tweet. But as with all the advice I've offered here, the effort is worthwhile to the extent that one cares about engaging readers in a respectful conversation about how to make the world a better place.

Social Media and Beyond

The Internet has changed how people think about public writing. Not that long ago, public writing was what appeared in books, newspapers, and magazines after passing through multiple editorial filters. There is still much of this kind of writing being done, for both print and online publication. Only writing that meets certain standards and follows the rules (see above) gets paid for, published, and made available to a wide audience. But now there are social media platforms that provide more options for public writing, along with more pitfalls.

Blogs are perhaps most like the old school method of self-publishing a magazine (or a 'zine), though many blogs are written by only one person. And just like magazines or 'zines, they can be well written and deal seriously with political and social matters of broad concern. The best blogs that I've seen tend to follow much of the writing advice that I've offered in this chapter.

What is great about these Internet-era options for public writing is that the barriers to participation are low. It isn't necessary to own a newspaper or a magazine or a TV station to get one's views out. Anyone who can afford a computer, or get access to one, can start a blog. Anyone with a cell phone can tweet. And there is little or no editorial filtering between writer and audience. All this is good in that it can enhance freedom of expression. Unfortunately, it isn't always conducive to mindful public writing.

Public writing is mindful, I've suggested, when it respects diverse readers, respects opponents, anticipates objections, and seeks to honestly inform. The problem is that social media hasn't required or encouraged any of this. Too often the tendency is to write for a group of like-minded others, in a mean or brash way about opponents, with little or no editorial filtering or prepublication feedback and revision. This kind of writing—a sharply barbed tweet is probably the best example—can make a writer feel good, yet not accomplish much. Or it may even backfire.

Another problem with many social media platforms is that they can limit thoughtfulness and serious analysis. Carefully examining a social problem, weighing evidence, making an argument, considering possible objections, and so on can't be done in 280 characters or a few sentences. It takes space. This isn't to say that a simple point can't be made in a tweet. It is to say that if we limit our public writing to tweets (or the equivalent), we will limit ourselves to saying simplistic things about matters that can't be fully understood without more complex, nuanced analysis.

The lack of editorial filtering, if only in the form of prepublication feedback, is yet another limitation of social media. While freedom of expression is generally good, failure to get feedback can lead to mistakes, obscurity, and inadvertent offensiveness. Lack of feedback also makes it hard to improve as a writer. So, when it comes to public writing, there is a downside to relying solely on social media. That's why I suggest trying to write, at least sometimes, for outlets that set high standards for accuracy and clarity.

Despite their limitations, social media can be powerful and empowering. These platforms can be used to share information and ideas and to coordinate action (see chapter 5 on organizing). Writing for social media can also be a way to hone one's ability to craft clear sentences that get to the point quickly. So, yes, writing for social media can be an important part of working for change. My point is that other kinds of public writing are needed as well.

I realize that not everyone can do the same kind of public writing. Not everyone has the same time, skills, and knowledge. Yet public writing, as I've tried to show, is more doable than many people—especially those who've suffered through writing assignments in school—might think. Any literate person who is willing to take a bit of care can do it. It's a way to contribute to a public conversation about solving social problems. It's a way, in other words, to help make the world a better place.

To Learn More

Becker, Howard S. (1986). *Writing for Social Scientists.* Chicago: University of Chicago Press.

Clark, Roy Peter. (2014). *How to Write Short: Word Craft for Fast Times.* New York: Little, Brown and Company.

Elbow, Peter. (1973). *Writing Without Teachers.* New York: Oxford University Press.

Goldberg, Natalie. (2016). *Writing Down the Bones: Freeing the Writer Within.* 30th Anniversary Edition. Boulder, CO: Shambhala Publications.

Graff, Gerald, and Birkenstein, Cathy. (2016). *They Say/I Say* (3rd ed.). New York: Norton.

Jensen, Robert. (2001). *Writing Dissent: Taking Radical Ideas from the Margins to the Mainstream.* New York: Peter Lang.

Lamott, Anne. (1994). *Bird by Bird: Some Instructions on Writing and Life.* New York: Pantheon.

Ueland, Brenda. (1987). *If You Want to Write: A Book about Art, Independence and Spirit.* Saint Paul, MN: Graywolf Press.

Zinsser, William. (1988). *Writing to Learn.* New York: Harper & Row.

Zinsser, William. (2013). *On Writing Well: The Classic Guide to Writing Nonfiction.* 30th Anniversary Edition. New York: Harper & Row.

CHAPTER 5
....

Organizing

I magine that you are having trouble with a boss. Maybe s/he is abusive or treats you and your co-workers unfairly. Or maybe there are problems with safety, pay, or scheduling. Any one employee who confronts the boss won't have much power. The boss can say, "If you don't like the situation, too bad. Find another job." But if all the employees confront the boss together, things are different. The balance of power changes because a boss can't fire everyone and keep a business going. In the face of organized resistance, the boss would have to listen and make changes.

To take another example, imagine that you and your neighbors are unhappy with local government. Maybe the city refuses to install stop signs to slow speeding traffic. Or maybe the city is permitting too much noisy commercial development nearby. Or maybe it's failing to repair school buildings. Again, a lone citizen who complains might not get much response. But if hundreds of people work together to hold public officials accountable for their actions and pressure them during elections, then the chances of getting a favorable response would be much greater.

These examples are about the power of organizing to make a difference in the world. It's not that we are always powerless as individuals; sometimes it's possible to speak out and get the people responsible for solving a problem to take action. But when the people who can solve a problem are in positions of power and have no interest in solving the problem—either because they benefit from it or have other priorities—organized action is necessary. In fact, historically, it has always been some kind of organized action that has done the most to make the world a better place.

One reason this isn't more widely recognized is that we're taught to think about social change as occurring through acts of moral heroism by extraordinary individuals. Susan B. Anthony, Rosa Parks, Martin Luther King Jr., Mohandas Gandhi, Nelson Mandela, and others are held up as the leaders without which great freedom struggles would not have been won. But as important as these people were, they did not make change on their own. Change was accomplished by the co-ordinated action of thousands (sometimes millions) of people, most of whom did a lot of mundane work behind the scenes. This is still how change occurs.

Another reason that organizing doesn't readily come to mind is that US labor history is not a required subject in school. In a US labor history course, students would learn that workers had to fight collectively, sometimes for years, to win victories over exploitive bosses, private police forces, and corrupt politicians. If more people were familiar with this history, they would know that making change does not depend on being a lone moral hero. They would know that making change—especially when people in power don't want it to happen—requires organizing.

In the simplest terms, organizing is just bringing people together to work in a coordinated way toward common goals. If the minds and muscle of many people are effectively coordinated, the ability to get things done is greatly magnified. In a sense, this is what power is: the ability to get things done, even in the face of obstacles. Organizing is thus a way for people to build power and accomplish things that no individual could accomplish on his or her own. It is how pyramids and fortunes are built.

Organizing is also how domination is accomplished, and how pyramids and fortunes are built on the backs of the powerless. This is not to say that organizing is good or bad; it depends on the moral value of the goals being pursued. But there is here a general sociological principle, which is this: the disorganized are vulnerable to domination by the organized. This is why people who want to make change in pursuit of social justice are often stymied. They are simply not as well organized as the powerful. Organizing is a way to balance the scales of power.

Sociologists are not professional organizers, but we do know a lot about how organizing is accomplished, including what works and what doesn't. This knowledge comes from studying social movements, grassroots community groups, and formal organizations (e.g., government agencies, corporations). It's possible, on the basis of this knowledge, to draw out principles and tips to help guide efforts to organize people seeking change. That's what I'll offer here, starting with principles. To learn more about the nuts and bolts of organizing, see the sources listed at the end of the chapter.

A Few (More) Principles

I have already noted a few key principles: organizing is how humans do things that are beyond the power of individuals, major social change occurs through organized collective action, the disorganized are vulnerable to domination by the organized, and organizing can reduce imbalances in power among groups in society. If not for these basic truths, there would be no point in writing about organizing as a way to make the world a better place. Which is why I needed to introduce these ideas first. There are, however, several more basic truths about organizing that are equally important to keep in mind.

Self-interest isn't necessarily selfish. Getting involved in an organizing effort usually means breaking from comfortable routines. This is one reason it can be hard to get people to participate, even when it seems that they should want to. Motivating people to get involved thus often requires convincing them that it's in their self-interest to do so. Appealing to the abstract goal of "achieving justice" is rarely enough. Most people, no matter how virtuous they are, won't dedicate themselves to the hard work of getting organized to make change happen unless there is something in it for them.

But doesn't appealing to self-interest encourage selfishness? Doesn't it encourage people to look out for themselves and avoid joining collective efforts to change things? Not necessarily, because many people's self-interests overlap. Recall the examples of the abusive boss and the unresponsive city government. In those cases, change would serve the interests of many people, and organized action would satisfy those interests better than individual action. This is what good organizers help people see—that getting involved in collective action can benefit them more than remaining aloof and apart.

People can of course get involved in organizing efforts for selfish reasons. Perhaps there is some interest—for money, status, or power—they are trying to satisfy solely for their own benefit. Or perhaps they hope to satisfy some interest of theirs at the expense of other people. These are possibilities. But if ordinary people organize to resist domination, or to address an injustice from which they all suffer, they are likely to be on guard against one person or a small faction trying to tilt the effort to their advantage. I'll say more later about how to guard against this problem.

The organizing process changes things. Ideally, organized action solves the problem that people aim to solve. Maybe the effort brings about passage of a new law, forces public officials to behave responsibly, changes the rules of a workplace, or gets a candidate elected to office. Whatever the outcome, success is apparent in having achieved the goal people set out to achieve. This kind of unequivocal success is what affirms people's trust in organizing as a way to make the world a better place.

Many times, however, the results are equivocal. Maybe the original goal is only partly achieved, or not achieved at all. Some people will look at these outcomes as failures. "See," they might say, "organizing doesn't really work—it wasn't worth the effort." But a good organizing effort, even if it doesn't achieve every goal, or seems like a failure, changes things. It changes relationships and people in ways that can matter later.

When people organize to resist being dominated or to challenge injustice, they learn that passive complaining is not their only option. They learn that their strength can be magnified by collective action, even if it turns out not to be enough strength to change everything they wanted to change. They learn how to work with others. In the process, they form friendships, invent new ideas, acquire skills, and gain confidence. These changes make people more ready and able to organize, more effectively, on later occasions. In these ways, organizing efforts today—whatever else their results—can foster change in the future.

Organizing doesn't require charisma. Famous leaders of social movements—people like Martin Luther King Jr. and Mohandas Gandhi—are often said to have possessed "charisma," a special gift for motivating and mobilizing followers. It seems clear that they did. But it is a mistake to think that organizing people requires a rare quality that is a gift from the gods. If we think this way, organizing for social change seems impossible without a charismatic leader to take charge. This is a paralyzing notion, one that can disempower people and impede change.

Organizing is in fact a skill, something that people can learn to do. It is what might be called a social technology. There are tools and techniques that have proven to be effective and can be learned. By mastering these tools and techniques, almost anyone can organize people to create change in the world. I don't mean to suggest that it's easy or that it doesn't require practice. But it's no less learnable than many other skills that ordinary people acquire in the course of their lives.

One more point: organizing is not the same as leading. Leading involves stirring emotions, articulating people's thoughts and desires, and offering inspiring visions of the future. Leading might also require the courage to get out in front of followers and take risks. Organizing, in contrast, involves getting people together and helping them coordinate their efforts to accomplish the practical tasks on which achieving change depends. It's true that sometimes leaders must organize and organizers must lead. But organizing is often distinct, occurring backstage, so to speak. If the work of organizing is done well, and the change effort succeeds, then perhaps in retrospect those who were in the spotlight on the front stage will be acclaimed as excellent leaders.

Sociologically Mindful Organizing

The best way to learn the skills of organizing is by working with experienced, successful organizers. Anyone wishing to become a good organizer should try to learn in this way. Most people, however, will not have a chance to apprentice with an experienced organizer before the need arises to organize. So there is a need for practical advice that anyone who wants to organize can use under most circumstances. That's what I'll offer here, drawing on sociological insights about why organizing efforts tend to fail or succeed.

The bits of advice that follow constitute what I am calling sociologically mindful organizing. This is not a special method but rather a way of paying attention to the organizing process that can keep it on track and keep it from falling apart. Successful organizers, in my experience, tend to be mindful of the matters identified below. To put it another way, successful organizers are often good applied sociologists, even if they don't wear that label.

Attend to feelings. Most people don't get involved in organizing efforts based solely on cost/benefit calculations. More likely, they are motivated by strong feelings—perhaps anger at unfairness, or fear of what might happen if a problem isn't addressed. Good organizers channel these feelings into constructive action. Good organizers also know that keeping people engaged means attending to their needs to feel respected and valued. Precisely how this needs to be done depends on the circumstances and the people involved. In general, however, when people feel disrespected or unappreciated, they are unlikely to stick around and contribute to a collective effort, so feelings can't be ignored. Feelings are part of what make us human, and no effort that ignores this part of our humanity is likely to succeed.

Listen. Active listening (see chapter 2) is one of an organizer's most important skills. To bring people together, it's essential to hear what they have to say. What problems do they have? What remedies do they seek? What kind of future do they want? Only by listening carefully to what people say about these matters is it possible to find the common ground on which people will work together for change. A good strategy, early in an organizing effort, is to ask people to tell stories about problems they've faced (or are currently facing). Stories are easier to tell and easier to absorb than "reports." Storytelling can also build trust and solidarity. But no matter how people share their experiences—by telling stories or in some other ways—listening is crucial. Not feeling listened to is another reason that people withdraw from efforts to organize.

Attend to diversity. People who face the same problem and have a shared interest in solving it might be quite different in other ways. There can be differences in values and outlook and style, perhaps related to social class, gender, sexuality, race, ethnicity, or age. A desire for harmony makes it tempting to ignore such differences. But if the differences are linked to unequal levels of privilege in society at large—for example, upper-middle-class white people generally being treated with more respect than working-class people of color—then they can't be ignored because they can undermine trust and solidarity. Good organizers therefore attend to diversity and try to build bridges of understanding among people who are differently located in society. Good organizers also look for ways to turn diversity into strength, using it to enhance creativity and build power by combining the complementary abilities of group members.

Conduct strategic research. Organizing efforts sometimes fail because people's complaints are dismissed as imaginary, or because the target of the effort is not the right person or agency. Strategic research is needed to avoid these problems. Gathering solid facts about the nature and extent of a problem is crucial. So is finding out who benefits from the status quo, who has the power (or official authority) to change it, who is likely to oppose change, and what the weaknesses of those opponents are. Knowledge of these matters is essential for devising effective strategies and tactics for pursuing change. Good organizers know that time spent doing research at the start of an organizing effort is not wasted. It increases the chances of success much like studying a map increases the chances of getting to one's desired destination on time.

Strategize and plan. To strategize is to formulate goals and identify broad types of action that can achieve those goals. Strategizing also takes into account resources, allies, opponents, and obstacles so as to develop an overview of the situation. Planning is more closely tied to action. It involves figuring out steps to take, who will take them, and when. Planning also includes thinking ahead about how to respond to opposition. It might seem obvious that any serious change effort needs to do these things. Yet oftentimes a desire to take immediate action will lead a group to forgo strategizing and planning. This can in turn lead a group to flounder after initial enthusiasm has waned. Strategizing and planning should not become ends in themselves; but without strategies and plans to guide action over the long haul, a change effort is likely to bog down. Good organizers thus devote time to strategizing and planning, knowing that strategies and plans can be revised as circumstances change.

Formulate process rules. Whenever people collaborate on complex projects, there is a need to determine how decisions will be made, who will be responsible for which tasks, how tasks will be assigned, who will be accountable to whom, who will speak for the group, and so on. Groups often operate poorly, or fall apart entirely, because these matters are not clearly resolved. To avoid confusion, conflict, and hurt feelings, process rules—rules about how the group is going to operate—need to be discussed and agreed on, the earlier the better. Such rules need not be elaborate, just adequate for the situation. Good organizers know that shared commitment to a set of democratically arrived at rules of procedure is the glue that holds groups together when the struggle for change puts people under stress.

Meet face to face. Electronic communication is great for sharing information and coordinating action. But it is not so great for attending to feelings, building trust, strategizing and planning, formulating rules of procedure, and making decisions democratically. These things are best done in person. To bridge differences, find common ground, and feel a sense of unity, people need to see and hear each other. This is how strong ties are formed—the ties that hold a group together during struggles to make change. Petition drives, letter-writing campaigns, and rallies can be organized through e-mail, texting, and social media. But these efforts are often ephemeral, evaporating quickly after some initial action is taken. Good organizers know that face-to-face meetings are better for building solidarity and securing commitment to a change effort.

Build coalitions. Part of strategizing is identifying allies—individuals, groups, and organizations that might join forces to support a change effort. Building a coalition means bringing these people, groups, and organizations together to share resources and coordinate action. "Resources" can include people, skills, money, knowledge, information, and contacts. What one group lacks, another might be able to provide. This is why good organizers look for new allies and ways to broaden a coalition. Just as bringing individuals together magnifies their power, bringing groups and organizations together magnifies this power even further. Although coalitions can thus bolster efforts to make change, they can also create new tensions. For this reason, it is important to formulate process rules (see above) about how members of a coalition will operate together.

Pick winnable battles. It's impossible to know ahead of time which battles are winnable. Historically, some battles that at first seemed unwinnable—obtaining the vote for women, overthrowing apartheid, abolishing slavery—were eventually won. In principle, any battle is winnable if enough people are well organized and willing to fight for as long as it takes. But most people, even if they agree that a problem exists and change is needed, are reluctant to join efforts to "overthrow the system," "abolish capitalism," or "create a just society." Such goals are too vague and grand. On the other hand, getting a new law enacted, electing a candidate, forming a union at work, or forcing government officials to fix a problem are more concrete goals that are potentially attainable within a reasonable period of time. It is thus easier to imagine winning these kinds of battles. Good organizers know that picking winnable battles with clear goals is important for recruiting people to a change effort and keeping them involved.

Be for something. Change efforts usually arise because an injustice needs to be rectified, or some form of abuse or exploitation needs to be ended. Anger about these problems and a desire to solve them can indeed be motivating. This is motivation that stems from people being against something. It is also good, however, to think about what a change effort is *for*, because this can speak to people's desires to help make the world a better place. For example, a corporation that dumps toxic waste into a creek that runs through a poor neighborhood gives people in that neighborhood something to fight against. But members of the wider community might join the effort if it is clear what the effort is for: lawful behavior, effective regulation, responsive government, a healthier environment. These are goals that most people will support. Being for something in this way can thus help bring more allies on board.

Be self-reflective. In all organizing efforts, some things go right and some things go wrong. There are successes and failures, and it's important to learn from both. Lessons can be drawn from carefully examining strategies, tactics, and procedures that work and those that don't. Being self-reflective is a matter of making time for this kind of examination, ensuring that the discussion is open to all participants, and taking it seriously. Groups that do this tend to learn from their mistakes and become stronger over time; groups that don't do it often fall apart. Constructive self-reflection isn't a matter of celebrating or blaming individuals. It should be an honest assessment of how well people worked together and how to do better the next time.

Seek knowledge about organizing. It's possible to learn about organizing through trial and error. Experience, when combined with self-reflection, is an excellent teacher. But this can be a slow and pain-ful way to learn. A better way is to draw on the body of knowledge that already exists. This knowledge can be found in books, schools, workshops, and people (see To Learn More). Drawing on this accumu-lated knowledge can make organizing efforts more effective and less likely to go awry. Even professional organizers, when facing unfamiliar circumstances, often call on more experienced organizers for advice. Good organizers, in other words, know when they need help—and ask for it. People who want to become organizers or who need to orga-nize, should tap the reservoirs of knowledge that have been created by others' experience and reflection.

A final point to bear in mind is that it isn't always necessary to or-ganize from scratch. Sometimes it is, if a new problem has arisen and people have not yet come together to deal with it. But often there are groups already organized to try to solve a social problem. Joining such a group, presuming that it functions reasonably well, can be a way to help make a difference and learn more about organizing (by seeing what works and what doesn't). Such efforts can also benefit greatly from the participation of people who know how to contribute in a sociologically mindful way.

Organizing as a Path to Mindfulness

People who read and write books tend to think that most things can be taught by writing books and learned by reading them. Of course, much can be taught and learned in this way. And it is a good thing, too, or else it would be much harder to transmit knowledge from one genera-tion to the next. But book knowledge (or "college knowledge," as I have also heard it called) doesn't always take deep root. This is because it is often detached from concrete experience.

The problem of book knowledge not sticking is as true of sociologi-cal mindfulness as it is of other matters. Without practical action to which such knowledge can be tied, it tends to slip away. Organizing, it seems to me, is precisely the kind of action that puts sociological mind-fulness to practical use and affirms its value. It is like the difference between learning botany from a textbook and putting that knowledge to use in a greenhouse or on a farm. It's the latter experience that brings the lessons to life and makes them stick.

I don't mean to suggest that organizing is an easy path to sociological mindfulness. Even with all the principles, advice, and wisdom in the world, organizing to oppose domination or injustice is a challenge. Resistance to change can be fierce. People seeking change can make bad mistakes. And even the best efforts don't always succeed, fully or partially. Yet every attempt, every success, every failure can teach a lesson. This is part of how organizing, as I said earlier, changes things. Organizing can indeed change the world. By getting together and deciding to resist being treated unfairly, people begin the process of change. By seeking common ground, overcoming differences, building mutual understanding, strategizing about what to do, recruiting allies, forming coalitions, and taking action, people become agents of history. When people are deeply involved in this kind of cooperative process, they gain new insight into how the social world works, becoming more sociologically mindful. What they also gain is new power to make the world a better place.

To Learn More

Alinsky, Saul D. (1971). *Rules for Radicals*. New York: Vintage.

Bobo, Kim, Kendall, Jackie, and Max, Steve. (2010). *Organizing for Social Change: Midwest Academy Manual for Activists* (4th ed.). Santa Ana, CA: The Forum Press.

Chenoweth, Erica, and Stephan, Maria J. (2011). *Why Civil Resistance Works: The Strategic Logic of Nonviolent Conflict*. New York: Columbia University Press.

Fantasia, Rick. (1988). *Cultures of Solidarity: Consciousness, Action, and Contemporary American Workers*. Berkeley: University of California Press.

Gecan, Michael. (2002). *Going Public: An Organizer's Guide to Citizen Action*. New York: Anchor.

Kahn, Si. (2010). *Creative Community Organizing: A Guide for Rabble Rousers, Activists, and Quiet Lovers of Justice*. San Francisco: Berrett-Koehler.

Moyer, Bill. (2001). *Doing Democracy*. Gabriola Island, BC: New Society Publishers.

Staples, Lee. (2004). *Roots to Power: A Manual for Grassroots Organizing* (2nd ed.). Westport, CT: Praeger.

Stout, Linda. (1996). *Bridging the Class Divide—And Other Lessons for Grassroots Organizing*. Boston: Beacon Press.

Stout, Linda. (2011). *Collective Visioning: How Groups Can Work Together for a Just and Sustainable Future*. San Francisco: Berrett-Koehler.

Stout, Jeffrey. (2010). *Blessed Are the Organized: Grassroots Democracy in America*. Princeton, NJ: Princeton University Press.

CHAPTER 6

Empathizing

One day in my social inequality class, we were discussing an article about economic hardships faced by women of color who were single mothers. A student, a white male in his early twenties, said, "If I were in that situation, I would just try harder to get ahead." This struck me as strange because the article stressed external obstacles to upward mobility, not lack of desire or effort. I was also struck by his presumption that everyone should be able to look at a situation of economic hardship in the same way that he would.

In response, I said that the article described the women as trying to get better jobs but being daunted by the costs of child care, lack of public transportation, too few educational opportunities, and discrimination in hiring—all matters beyond their control. Then I asked him a question. Do you suppose, I said, that emotions affect how we behave? The answer was so obvious that the student paused before saying yes. This gave me an opening to say that it's always a good idea, when wondering about someone else's behavior, to imagine how they perceive and feel about their circumstances.

The student in this case was fully capable, as he showed in other ways during the semester, of discerning facts and using complex ideas to analyze those facts. But what he often suffered from, as evident in his try-harder remark, was a failure of empathy—an inability to see things from others' perspectives. This was not an idiosyncratic personality defect that affected him alone. The problem is common and socially patterned.

Many of us make a similar kind of mistake. When looking at someone else's misbehavior, we tend to overattribute it to personality. When looking at our own misbehavior, we tend to overattribute it to circumstance. This is a such a common form of cognitive bias that social psychologists call it the "fundamental attribution error." We might also call it a failure to empathize.

When I say that the failure to empathize is socially patterned, I mean that it is predictably associated with certain social conditions. For instance, empathy tends to decrease as social distance increases. The farther apart people are socially, the harder it is for them to see the world through each other's eyes. Social distance is the kind created by differences in race, ethnicity, gender, class, religion, sexuality, ability/disability, nationality, and age. Along these social lines, people can be near to each other or far apart. They can also be near in some ways and far apart in others.

Another pattern is for empathy to decrease as power increases. More precisely, it is *having power* that tends to impede empathizing. This is usually explained by noting that the powerful have less incentive to take the perspectives of the powerless than vice versa. After all, if you're powerless and vulnerable, your survival can depend on being able to figure out what the powerful are thinking, feeling, and likely to do. In contrast, the powerful don't have to worry as much about what the powerless are thinking and feeling.

Another obstacle to empathizing is tribalism. This might sound strange, since we usually associate tribes with pre-industrial societies. But even in the modern technological world, we can live in the equivalent of tribes. These are the groups in which we anchor our identities, the groups to which we belong that give us a sense of being different from everyone else. The tribe is *us*; outsiders are *them*. Tribes in this sense can form based on the social categories I mentioned earlier: race, ethnicity, gender, class, religion, sexuality, ability/disability, nationality, and age.

Belonging to a group of others with whom we identify can be a good thing. We are social creatures, and belonging to groups and communities is how we become and remain human. Members of tribes also tend to support each other in times of adversity. So tribal feeling isn't always bad. A problem arises, however, when people begin to think that the values and beliefs of their tribe are only good values and true beliefs. By implication, outsiders who value and believe different things are lost in error, and perhaps morally and intellectually inferior. In which case, they are either irrational and impossible to understand or not worth the effort. Members of other tribes might even come to be seen as less than human.

Why does any of this matter? So what if social distance, inequalities in power, and tribalism impede empathy? The answer has to do with the consequences of failing to empathize, or failing to empathize beyond our group. Such failure tends to create, or allow to persist, much suffering in the world. A failure of empathy can also make it harder to solve social problems.

Empathy, Understanding, and Analysis

Analysis of how the social world works can be thwarted by a failure to empathize. Recall the student who seemed to think that, to better their lives, low-income women of color with children just needed to try harder. The efforts the women were already making, the obstacles that kept them from getting ahead, and the suffering they experienced were invisible to him. So, from his perspective, there wasn't much of a problem to be investigated and analyzed. After saying, "try harder," he felt no need to do more thinking.

If we would like to make the world a better place by reducing suffering and solving social problems, we need to be on guard against failures of empathy that lead to failures of analysis. Here is another example. This one is fictitious, but it closely tracks what we know based on years of research about success in school.

Suppose that there is an "achievement gap" in school between kids from poor families and kids from middle-class families. We see that kids from poor families, even if they're no less smart, don't do as well in school as kids from middle-class families. If we wanted to close this gap, we would have to find out what is causing it. There are many variables we might look at, but one thing is for sure: we would have to take into account how kids perceive and feel about school because this will affect their motivation and how well they get along with teachers.

What we might find is that kids from middle-class families feel more at ease in school because the middle-class teachers remind these kids of their parents and other adults in their lives. Perhaps they perceive teachers as taking an interest in them and providing support. Perhaps they look at the middle-class adults in their lives and see that school is likely to pay off. So these kids don't perceive school as a threat to their dignity, and they see it as likely to yield benefits in the long run. It would make sense, then, that middle-class kids, on average, would have more nurturing experiences in school and be more motivated to do well.

Kids from poor families, in contrast, might feel less at ease in school because unfamiliar people are in charge. Perhaps they perceive teachers mainly as disciplinarians who, if they aren't delivering a scolding, take little interest in them. Kids from poor families might also have fewer adults in their lives who exemplify how schooling pays off. So these kids perceive school as a place that threatens their dignity and ensures no rewards. It would make sense, then, that kids from poor families, on average, would have less nurturing experiences in school and be less motivated to do well.

The point of this example is that to analyze a social problem, we have to explore the perspectives of the people involved. In the case of the achievement gap, we would need to explore the perspectives of poor and middle-class students to understand how their experiences of school differ and how this might affect their success. We would also want to explore the perspectives of teachers. It would be impossible to understand what's going on, let alone devise a solution, without doing this. A good analysis, in other words, would require empathizing.

Here is another kind of example, one that is closer to what sometimes happens when we talk about social problems in everyday life. In this case, the failure to empathize arises from what might be called political tribalism. What this failure keeps us from doing is talking to each other in ways that move us toward a better understanding of a problem and what to do about it.

Imagine that someone said, "As a conservative, I don't believe in climate change." Such a statement implies that identifying with a political group dictates what one takes to be true about reality. This differs from tying a political philosophy (e.g., conservatism) to a preference (e.g., for smaller government). The latter makes sense; preferences *should* arise from well-considered philosophies. But to make acceptance of empirical claims—claims that can be tested through careful study—dependent on a political identity is to embrace trib-alism. It doesn't matter what the identity might be. If someone said, "As a liberal, I believe that gun control saves lives," the error would be the same.

There is, of course, nothing wrong with thinking of oneself as a liberal, conservative, radical, democrat, republican, libertarian, anar-chist, or anything else. This in itself isn't a problem. It's when allegiance to an identity interferes with honest fact seeking that a problem arises. This makes it hard to arrive at an accurate, shared understanding of what's going on and what we might do about it. So embracing political identities is fine provided that we remain open to seeking and facing facts arrived at through sound research.

Empathizing isn't just about how nice we are to the other people with whom we interact in everyday life. It's also about how well we are able, as members of a large and diverse society, to understand each other; how well we are able to see suffering that needs to be al-leviated; and how well we are able to talk to each other and apply our collective intelligence to solving common problems. If we can't do these things, then we're going to have a hard time creating a better world. So, somehow, we have to find ways to avoid failures of empa-thy. Awareness of the external conditions—social distance, inequal-ity, tribalism—that cause these failures is a start. The next step is to find ways around the barriers that these conditions create in our minds.

Overcoming Barriers in Mind

Perhaps in the long run we can eliminate the social conditions that create barriers to empathy. In the short run, we need strategies that can be used in everyday life to improve our abilities to empathize. The strategies I'm going to suggest are aimed at changing the habits of mind that impede empathizing. If we become aware of these habits, we can work around them and perhaps form new habits. Here are some sug-gestions for how to do this.

Put yourself aside. The student who thought low-income women of color with children could solve their problems by trying harder did not put himself aside when thinking about the circumstances these women face. When he said, "If I were in that situation, I would just try harder," he was imagining himself—with his accumulated resources and the benefits of being a white male—in a different situation. He was not imagining what it would be like to be a woman of color with few resources and options, coping with racism and sexism, while also trying to raise children. His habit of mind was to project himself into the situation of an other, rather than to imagine what it would be like to be the other.

It's impossible, of course, to fully understand how others experience their circumstances. We can go only so far in doing this before we reach the limits of our imagination. To expect a white male college student in his early twenties to be able to inhabit the perspective of a low-income woman of color with children is unfair. Still, he could have gone further had he put himself aside for a moment. Instead of thinking about what he would do under tougher circumstances, he might have asked, What would it be like to be her, with a different biography and fewer resources, in that situation? This strategy would have extended his empathetic reach.

Many of us fail to put ourselves aside when trying to understand others' experiences. As I argued earlier, the more different the other, the more likely we are to fail. But being aware of this tendency can help us overcome it. We can catch ourselves when we think only about what we would do in an other's circumstances. If we can take the next step and try to imagine what it would be like to be the other, we will come closer to achieving the level of understanding necessary to help alleviate their suffering.

Consider differences in biography and social position. By "social position" I mean where a person or group stands in relation to other persons or groups along the lines of wealth, status, and power. This kind of positioning can deeply affect people's perspectives (though not always in obvious or straightforward ways). Pausing to consider how this might be the case is a step toward better empathizing. A way to take this step is to ask, How might people in this group or category, given that they have historically experienced much greater/much lesser wealth, status, and power than members of my group, see things differently? Just asking this question can alert us to the need for more imaginative effort.

It is also important to consider individual biographies. This means trying to understand how a person's life experiences—especially those related to membership in a dominant or subordinate group—have shaped his or her perspective. Whatever understandings we arrive at will always be incomplete. But acknowledging that someone else's life experiences, perhaps very different from ours, have instilled different beliefs, values, and feelings is a step toward better empathizing. We can't make the imaginative effort if we fail to appreciate the need to do so.

Consider similarity. I have just stressed the need to acknowledge difference, so it might seem strange to say that we should consider similarity. But this, too, is an important step. What it entails is recognizing our common humanity. Otherwise, we might end up thinking that people are so different from us that we can't understand them. Considering similarity is a way to bridge the differences that we initially acknowledge.

Some things are common to people everywhere: love for one's family members; love for one's spouse or partner; pleasure in play, creative work, sex, eating; a desire to avoid pain and hunger; anger at being abused; a desire for purpose and respect; a desire to be treated fairly. Considering these similarities reminds us that, whatever our differences, our basic human needs and desires are much the same. This similarity provides a foundation for empathizing across lines of difference. Even when considering those differences, we need to remember that there is a deeper foundation on which we can build understanding.

Beware of tribal language. Tribal language is language that casts groups of people as different in some way that makes them inferior—intellectually, morally, or both—to members of one's own group. The most common examples in US culture are racial slurs. So are terms such as "hillbilly" or "white trash." These terms diminish the humanity of others and make them seem less deserving of being understood. Tribal language can even give us a false sense of understanding others—by implying that we all know what *those people* are like—when in fact we haven't made any effort to see the world through their eyes.

As I noted earlier, tribal language often appears in political discourse. People who might believe different things and hold diverse, thoughtful positions, are lumped together—and their views ignored or dismissed—under labels such as "liberal," "conservative," "radical," "reactionary," and so on. In such cases, tribal language is being used to stifle conversation. If we see this happening, we can resist by asking, What are the values and beliefs behind the labels? Why do these values and beliefs seem right to others? These questions remind us that others deserve our efforts to empathize with them, even if we don't accept their values and beliefs.

Perhaps the most damaging use of tribal language occurs in times of war. Terms such as "gooks" and "slopes" reduce others to subhuman status and make it easier to harm them. Terms such as "targets," "terrorists," or "collateral damage" have the same effect: they turn human beings into objects that have no feelings worth considering. When we encounter these dehumanizing terms we should remember that the people being talked about are mothers, fathers, sons, daughters, sisters, and brothers—just like us. Creating a more peaceful world depends on rejecting the empathy-killing language used by those who seek to justify violence.

Listen and read. I have referred to empathizing—putting ourselves in the shoes of the other, so to speak—as requiring acts of imagination. But we must do more than imagine. We must also listen (see chapter 2). Others often tell us what the world looks like to them and how they experience it. Listening to what they tell us, taking seriously what they say, is how we learn to accurately imagine what it's like to be them. To better empathize, we must guard against the habit of failing to listen. It is especially important to do this when we encounter values and beliefs that are different from our own.

Unfortunately, we might rarely, if ever, meet people whose experiences and perspectives are really different from our own. If we spend all our time with people who are like us, we might never have an honest conversation with someone who is different. The "try harder" student in my class probably had never talked to a low-income woman of color trying to raise children on her own. This kind of social insulation is one reason we rely on stereotypes to know about others, though this usually means that much of what we think we know is wrong. Fortunately, we can begin to work around this problem by reading.

Like talking and listening, reading is a way to get inside the minds of others. We can gain access to their thoughts by reading their autobiographies and memoirs. These kinds of texts are great tools for understanding how others' experiences and perspectives differ from ours. Works of fiction—short stories and novels—are also valuable. When we are caught up in a story by a good writer, it is easier to put ourselves aside and imaginarily inhabit the worlds of others. This experience shrinks social distance and nurtures our ability to empathize. My advice, then, is simple: read as much fiction and nonfiction written by and about unfamiliar others as you can. Sometimes helping to make the world a better place can be accomplished, if only in a small way, by opening a book.

Mindfully Pausing on the Way to Doing

The "try harder" student whom I've used as an example in this chapter was not resistant to empathizing. He just didn't pause to make the effort and instead rushed to judgment. When I slowed him down and pointed out that he'd missed key parts of the article he'd read (or read hastily), and said that a good analysis of the women's situation required seeing things from their perspective, he agreed. What I did, as his teacher, was help him be more sociologically mindful by paying attention to things he should have paid attention to himself.

Much of being sociologically mindful amounts to pausing to pay attention to things that we know, on reflection, are important. But if we have learned the habits of rushing, of relying on stereotypes, of not listening carefully, of impulsively justifying ourselves and judging others, then mindfulness eludes us. So what I have been urging here is taking time to try to see how others who are different from us perceive and feel about the world. Just as we make mistakes in other activities when we rush and act as if we know more than we do, we make mistakes in understanding others when we rush and act as if we know more than we do. Pausing to empathize is a way to avoid, as much as we ever can, these kinds of mistakes.

When we fail to empathize, we are also likely to make mistakes in analysis. To understand why people do what they do, we must take their perceptions and feelings into account. Empathizing is how we do this. It's part of figuring out what's going on in the world, why the social world keeps going as it does, and how we might change it. This is why, if we want to make the world a better place, we need to do better at empathizing, especially across lines of difference.

If making the world a better place includes reducing people's suffering, then empathizing is necessary to understand the suffering that needs to be alleviated. Failures of empathy can lead us to believe that everything is fine and nothing needs changing. By empathizing, we experience compassion for others and learn, perhaps, that everything is not fine for everyone. So pausing to empathize is not only for the sake of analysis. It's also for appreciating the need for change and, later, for talking about how to pursue it peacefully.

I've written about empathizing as a kind of mental practice through which we can better understand others. This is indeed what empathizing mainly involves; it is a kind of thinking aided by acts of communication—listening, reading, talking. The point, however, is not simply to better understand others and store this knowledge in our heads; the point is to act more intelligently and compassionately when facing social problems. Empathizing might not tell us exactly what to do, but if it leads us to see and feel strongly that something needs to be done, it will move us along the path to creating a better world.

To Learn More

Baron-Cohen, Simon. (2011). *The Science of Evil: On Empathy and Origins of Cruelty*. New York: Basic Books.

Beam, Cris. (2018). *I Feel You: The Surprising Power of Extreme Empathy*. Boston: Houghton Mifflin Harcourt.

Coplan, Amy, and Goldie, Peter (eds.). (2011). *Empathy: Philosophical and Psychological Perspectives*. New York: Oxford University Press.

Franks, David D. (1985). "Role-Taking, Social Power, and Imperceptiveness: The Analysis of Rape." *Studies in Symbolic Interaction* 6: 229–259.

Iacoboni, Marco. (2009). *Mirroring People: The Science of Empathy and How We Connect with Others*. New York: Picador.

Keen, Suzanne. (2010). *Empathy and the Novel*. New York: Oxford University Press.

McLaren, Karen. (2013). *The Art of Empathy: A Complete Guide to Life's Most Essential Skill*. Louisville, CO: Sounds True.

Noddings, Nel. (2013). *Caring: A Relational Approach to Ethics and Moral Education* (2nd. ed.). Berkeley: University of California Press.

Rifkin, Jeremy. (2009). *The Empathic Civilization: The Race to Global Consciousness in a World in Crisis.* New York: TarcherPerigee/Penguin.

Schwalbe, Michael L. (1988). "Role-Taking Reconsidered: Linking Competence and Performance to Social Structure." *Journal for the Theory of Social Behavior* 19(4): 411–436.

Thomas, Darwin L., Franks, David D., and Calonico, James. (1972). "Role-Taking and Power in Social Psychology." *American Sociological Review* 37(5): 604–614.

CHAPTER 7

Advocating

When I was a kid, there were ads on the bus that showed a light-skinned male hand holding a college diploma. The caption below the image said, TO GET A GOOD JOB, GET A GOOD EDUCATION. That's still sound advice. A college degree doesn't guarantee getting a good job, but it greatly improves the odds. Many employers want people with the skills that higher education imparts: excellent reading comprehension, the ability to find and analyze information, and the ability to write well. Acquiring these skills is not easy. Which is one reason that only about a third of US adults have a college degree.

We usually think of attending a college or university as something we do not only to boost our career prospects but also to discover new interests, to develop our potentials, and to acquire knowledge that helps us understand and appreciate the world more fully. In these ways, higher education equips us to get more out of life for ourselves. There is nothing wrong with this; it's reasonable to expect some kind of return for the time and effort we put into learning. But perhaps, if we want to make the world a better place, we should think of this "return" in broader terms.

Imagine a modern society in which only one percent of the adults had college degrees. If this were the case, it's likely that power—control of the economy, government, and other major institutions—would be concentrated in the hands of the educated few. Most people would be unequipped to participate in running society, and democracy would be impossible. Now imagine a society in which all the adults had benefit of higher education. In this case, it would be much harder for elites to monopolize power. Nearly everyone would be equipped to participate in running society; and, although not ensured, democracy would be much more possible.

What does this thought experiment suggest about the United States as it really is? Perhaps that those who are fortunate enough to acquire the skills that enable participation in running society have an important role to play when it comes to finding democratic solutions to social problems. Consider, too, that much of the suffering caused by social problems is borne by those who are least well equipped, at least by formal education, to challenge elites for power and pursue solutions that serve the common good. This condition further suggests a special role, or special obligation, for the beneficiaries of higher education when it comes to making the world a better place.

One way to play this role is by advocating. By this I mean using one's skills and knowledge to help change the laws and policies that cause others to suffer unfairly. In a competitive and individualistic society, we often feel pressure to do the opposite: to take action only when we will benefit. Of course we need to look out for our own interests, and there is nothing wrong with doing so provided that it doesn't harm others. But if we want to make the world a better place for everyone, including ourselves, we need to look beyond our narrow self-interests.

Advocating does not require a college degree. Anyone who works on behalf of others who are more vulnerable and more directly harmed by a problem is acting as an advocate. Still, the knowledge and skills conferred by higher education offer a clear advantage in this kind of change-making activity. This is one reason I've connected higher education to advocating. Another reason is that most readers will encounter this book in a college course, on their way to acquiring resources that most Americans lack. If such relatively privileged readers then ask, *What can we do to help solve the problems that our education brings to light?*, one especially fitting answer is "advocating."

I am not suggesting that an educated minority should presume to know how best to solve other people's problems. This sort of presumptuousness is a potential downside to higher education (or, really, to the unequal distribution of higher education). I'll say more later about how advocates can avoid this problem. For now, I want to make the point that advocating does not mean "taking charge" or claiming the authority to speak for others. It means adding one's strength to efforts to reduce the suffering of others, in a way that best suits one's abilities, without diminishing the dignity of those being helped.

Some readers might be familiar with the idea of "being an ally," which perhaps seems much like what I am calling advocating. The two ideas are indeed closely related, though they're not quite the same. By distinguishing them, it is possible to see different ways that one can contribute to making the world a better place by working on behalf of others. While we all can be allies at key moments, being an advocate implies something more.

Allies and Advocates

Both allyship and advocacy can help resist injustice and reduce suffering, and both practices are important. The main difference, as I see it, is that advocating means working in the public sphere to change laws and policies that are unjust and/or cause surplus suffering, whereas allyship usually occurs out of the public eye. In this sense, all advocates are allies, but not all allies engage in public advocacy. Because both practices are important and because the distinction I'm drawing might seem a bit abstract, I'll offer examples of each.

Examples of Allyship

Allies are members of privileged groups who seek to change the cultural beliefs and practices that give them those privileges. As a matter of principle, allies believe that it is wrong for some people to enjoy higher status, fairer treatment, or more opportunities in life simply because of the social group or category to which they belong. And so, when appropriate occasions arise, allies try to break the patterns of everyday behavior that reinforce inequality. They try to ensure that members of marginalized, devalued, or subordinated groups are afforded equal status, fair treatment, and equal opportunities.

Many examples of allyship come from organizational life. Imagine a meeting in which most of the powerful actors are white males. Because of how racist and sexist biases can operate both consciously and unconsciously, it would not be surprising if a young woman of color struggled to be heard and taken seriously in this situation. A white male who saw this happening and intervened, making sure that the young woman's ideas were given a fair hearing, would be acting as an ally. If, in a different situation, the same white male challenged racist and sexist joking among his white male peers, this would be another example of allyship. Still another example would be reaching out and offering mentorship to people, such as women of color, who had historically been excluded from leadership positions in the organization.

For most members of dominant groups, everyday life provides plenty of chances to act as allies. Whenever members of less privileged groups are disrespected, mistreated, or unfairly excluded from opportunities, allies can speak up and say that this is wrong. This might seem like a simple matter of being a decent person. What makes allyship hard is that it means challenging the biases and discriminatory behavior of people in dominant groups. But this is precisely what allies are best positioned to do, and it's the insider status of allies that makes their actions so powerful.

Examples of Advocating

Whereas allyship usually involves interpersonal intervention, as suggested by the preceding examples, advocacy involves intervention in more public processes, such as policy debates, elections, and organizing campaigns. The goal of advocating is to change not just individual behavior but the social conditions that affect the lives of many people. Like other allies, advocates believe in fairness for all and try to use their knowledge, skills, and other resources to reduce the suffering experienced by less powerful, less privileged others.

For example, suppose that state legislators want to create a lottery as a way to raise revenues. An upper-middle-class person with a high income might think this is fine. It will keep his or her taxes low, and it will be mostly people with lower incomes—people hoping, against enormous odds, for a big win—who buy lottery tickets. But another upper-middle-class person might see the unfairness in a lottery system, precisely because, as a tax in disguise, it puts a heavier burden on those less able to afford it. If this person publicly opposed the lottery—by signing petitions; writing letters to the editor, op-eds, or blog posts; e-mailing legislators; or attending rallies—this would constitute advocating.

Imagine, for another example, an upper-middle-class person who is white and lives in a safe, affluent suburb. For this person and his or her family members, the likelihood of suffering violence at the hands of police is low. And so the issue of police violence, when raised by black activists in an inner-city area, might seem remote and be easy to ignore. But if this same person took the issue seriously and publicly supported efforts to reform police training (to teach de-escalation rather than intimidation), to establish citizen review boards to monitor police behavior, and to change laws that protect police from the consequences of misbehavior, s/he would be an advocate.

One more example: imagine that state legislators are proposing to enact a law that will require new forms of identification before people are allowed to vote. Previous experience shows that such a law will make it harder for poor people, the elderly, the disabled, and college students to vote, thus lowering their participation—which is perhaps the goal that some legislators are aiming for. A person who would not be much affected by the law might shrug and take no action. Another person who likewise would not be affected might nonetheless believe that voting is a right and should be made as easy as possible for everyone. This person could become an advocate by publicly opposing passage of the new law, in the ways noted above.

These examples of advocating are not far-fetched; they exist in the real world: men who advocate for change that will benefit women; whites who advocate for change that will benefit people of color; able-bodied people who advocate for change that will benefit the disabled; wealthy people who advocate for change that will benefit the poor. And so on. Many people who are not directly hurt by a policy or practice— and might even benefit from it—try to make change that will improve life for others. These are the ways in which advocates can make the world a better place.

Sociologically Mindful Advocacy

Like all the change-making practices described in this book, advocating can be done in more or less effective ways. We can accomplish more, I think, by using the findings and methods of sociology to analyze social problems (see chapter 3 on researching) and by being sociologically mindful when we act as advocates. Allyship, too, can benefit from being done in a sociologically mindful way. So whether one aims to interrupt the reproduction of inequality through quiet, backstage interventions, or through vocal public ones, here are some suggestions for how to do this work more effectively.

Take time to listen and learn. Being an advocate requires understanding the circumstances and experiences of others. How does some policy or practice affect them? What is the problem they face? How does a policy or practice create this problem? It takes effort to find good answers to these questions; and for this purpose, listening, empathizing, and researching are essential. One danger of higher education, as I noted earlier, is that it can lead advocates to think they know more than they do and thus to jump in prematurely and unhelpfully. Advocates who take time to study an issue—to gather facts and to respect the knowledge of those whom they would presume to help—will be able to speak with more credibility and force.

Consider your sphere of influence. It's fine to speak out about big issues—military spending, foreign trade, climate change, war. Advocating in regard to these issues is important and can make a difference. But often we can have a greater effect if we speak to issues closer to home. Our neighbors and local politicians are more likely to care what we think and to listen to us than people who are more distant. So when considering how best to use the limited time available for advocating, it is wise to think about where we are likely to have the most influence. We should also bear in mind that acting locally can produce effects that ripple outward and create farther-reaching change (see chapter 12).

Speak to common interests. An affluent white suburbanite who advocates to reduce police violence could cite the suffering of inner-city residents most likely to be hurt. Another approach would be to say that we all have an interest in seeing that police officers are well trained, professional, and not prone to unwarranted violence because we all might need to call on the police for help, and because more crimes will be solved if everyone feels that they can trust the police. Even the police could benefit from more trust and less tension when doing their jobs in economically distressed areas. Looked at this way, we can see that there is a common interest at stake; the community as a whole could benefit from police reform. This approach to advocating—helping people see their common interests—is crucial to mobilizing broad support for change.

Learn from mistakes. Advocating often entails leaving one's comfort zone. It takes time and effort to learn and listen, and listening can mean hearing some troubling things (e.g., how members of one's own group are responsible for a problem). Speaking out about a problem suffered by the less powerful can incur the wrath of the more powerful. Speaking out before doing the research and listening necessary to understand a problem, or speaking with unearned authority, might be criticized by the people one is trying to help. It's possible, in other words, to get flak for trying to do a good thing. What's important is not to let discomfort or fear of making mistakes become a barrier to advocating. Discomfort and mistakes are parts of the process. Learning from these experiences is how we become better advocates.

Speak to other members of one's group. Unfortunately, the knowledge and experience of people who suffer from a problem are often discounted by members of dominant or privileged groups. Reports from people who suffer the most are seen as biased or as whining. Here is where advocates, presuming that they have done the necessary listening and learning, can help. Advocates, like allies, can make it a point to speak to other members of their group. Sometimes this is what gets a message across because the advocate is not dismissed as "having an axe to grind." Helping other members of a dominant or privileged group understand the seriousness of a problem is an especially powerful role for advocates to play.

Amplify others' voices. If the people hurt by a problem are marginalized or relatively powerless, they can have a hard time being heard. Advocates can help by taking what needs to be heard and conveying it to other members of dominant and privileged groups. They can also try to create platforms and opportunities for those who are hurt to be heard. This could mean providing opportunities to speak at panels, conferences, or group meetings, or opportunities to publish. It depends on what a person who wants to be an advocate can do. As I said when I wrote about empathizing (see chapter 6), social problems can't be understood, let alone solved, unless the perspectives of the people affected are taken into account. Advocates can try to make sure that this happens.

Seek solutions, not praise. Being an advocate might earn us praise for being willing to strive for justice on behalf of less-powerful others. Such praise is of course rewarding; it makes us feel virtuous and appreciated. But advocacy driven mainly by a desire for these kinds of rewards is not likely to last long. The sustained commitment necessary to create social change is more likely to arise from a desire to end the injustice and suffering that motivated the change effort originally—a desire to find solutions. Effective advocates, to put it another way, learn to keep their eyes on the prize, not the praise.

Advocating in Concert with Others

Although it's possible to act as an advocate without joining a group or consulting with anyone else, this is probably not the best way to go. When trying to learn about a problem, it helps to connect with others who are already knowledgeable, and especially with those who experience the problem. Others who are already working to find solutions to a problem may also know what kind of advocating is most needed at any given time. We can then coordinate our action with theirs so that efforts are not duplicated, and we can make a more useful contribution.

Advocating can also be emotionally taxing. It can mean facing disapproval, puzzlement, or indifference from family, friends, and other members of the groups and categories to which we belong. They might say to us, *This isn't your fight. Why are you taking up this issue? Leave it alone. Stop bugging us about it.* Such responses can be discouraging. This is another reason it helps to connect with people who are already working on a problem. It is through such connections that we gain the moral and emotional support necessary to carry on the work of advocating. We can also provide this kind of support to others.

Another reason for working with others is that advocating aims at changing social conditions, changing laws or policies, changing widespread cultural practices, or all of these. As I said in chapter 5 on organizing, these are not the kinds of changes we can make on our own. We can sometimes spark or catalyze change through what we do individually, but changing how society operates requires collective action. This is especially true when change threatens privileged or powerful groups. In such cases, adding our voices to those of others is likely to be more effective, and make us less vulnerable, than speaking out alone. In writing about organizing, I also said that a campaign for change can be successful even if every goal isn't met. Successes can include gains in organizing skills, new relationships of solidarity, and deeper commitments to seeking justice. The same is true of advocating. By learning to advocate well in regard to one issue, we gain the ability to advocate more effectively on other issues. By advocating in concert with others, we learn the value of organizing, and perhaps also form relationships that will sustain our commitments to future struggles to reduce the suffering of others. So advocating, like organizing, can produce changes in the present that will enable greater changes later.

Advocating can also promote change because it is a powerful form of teaching by example (see chapter 9). One person's acts of advocacy can inspire others to become advocates. One person's acts of advocacy show that all people in a privileged group are not the enemies of justice. One person's acts of advocacy show that it is possible for people of conscience in all groups to find common ground on which to work together for change. When advocates exemplify this possibility through their actions, they fuel the hope that keeps people engaged in trying to make the world a better place.

To Learn More

Bishop, Anne. (2015). *Becoming an Ally* (3rd ed.). Black Point, NS: Fernwood Publishing.

Cohen, David, de la Vega, Rosa, and Watson, Gabrielle. (2001). *Advocacy for Social Justice: A Global Action and Reflection Guide*. Sterling, VA: Kumarian Press.

Collins, Chuck. (2016). *Born on Third Base: A One Percenter Makes the Case for Tackling Inequality, Bringing Wealth Home, and Committing to the Common Good*. White River Junction, VT: Chelsea Green Publishing.

Craigo-Snell, Shannon, and Doucot, Christopher. (2017). *No Innocent Bystanders: Becoming an Ally in the Struggle for Justice*. Louisville, KY: Westminster John Knox Press.

Daly, John. A. (2012). *Advocacy: Championing Ideas and Influencing Others*. New Haven, CT: Yale University Press.

Hoefer, Richard. (2015). *Advocacy Practice for Social Justice* (3rd ed.). New York: Oxford University Press.

Jensen, Robert. (2005). *The Heart of Whiteness: Confronting Race, Racism, and White Privilege*. San Francisco: City Lights Publishers.

Katz, Jackson. (2006). *The Macho Paradox: Why Some Men Hurt Women and How All Men Can Help*. Naperville, IL: Sourcebooks.

Kivel, Paul. (2017). *Uprooting Racism: How White People Can Work for Racial Justice* (4th ed.). Gabriola Island, BC: New Society Publishers.

CHAPTER 8

Conserving

People who are unfamiliar with academic life often think there is something inherently radical about doing science or scholarship. Yes, individual scientists and scholars (who are often professors) might embrace radical perspectives, political or intellectual. But the work itself—the way it's actually done—is based on belief in the value of conserving. So, strange as it might seem, even the most politically or intellectually radical scientists and scholars are conservatives of a kind.

One of the tips I offered about researching (see chapter 3) was to start with what's already known. I said that this is what scientists and scholars routinely do. Before launching a study, they review the literature to find out what others have found previously. They might be skeptical about the methods, findings, or interpretations of their colleagues. They might think that previous work is flawed in some way. But the previous work isn't ignored; it's built on. That's a form of conserving.

The kind of conserving I'm referring to—building on the past—is often obscured by emphasizing the new. After all, that's what science and scholarship are supposed to produce: new findings, new concepts, new theories. The new is what matters, and so it gets the spotlight. But of course the new is findable only because knowledge of what's been done before has been conserved. The tricky part is figuring out what should be conserved and what should be discarded or revised. When we figure this out, it's fair to say that we've made progress.

We face a similar problem in everyday life. We encounter new facts and ideas, and then we must decide how to revise our current knowledge. Usually, we don't want to hold on to what's old if it's clear—perhaps by performing some sort of experiment—that new ideas do a better job of explaining what we observe, or if new facts are more accurate and precise. At the same time, we don't want to throw out what's old just because what's new seems hip or chic. So, like scientists and scholars, we have to figure out what's worth conserving and what's not.

The problem of deciding what to conserve goes beyond science, scholarship, and common sense; it's not just a matter of knowledge but also of practices—the ways of doing things together to which we have become accustomed—and of material conditions: nature and the built environment. As we age, we are often asked to give up old, familiar practices in favor of new ones. Nature and the built environment are also constantly threatened or altered. In these matters, too, we must decide what to try conserving and what to let go.

It might seem odd, in a book about making change, to dwell on conserving, since conserving seems like resisting change. But making the world a better place doesn't mean seeking change for change's sake. It means trying to create a world in which there is more opportunity and less discrimination, more peace and less violence, more equality and less poverty, more democracy and less domination, more joy and less suffering. If this is what we mean by a better world, then we need to evaluate the likely consequences of proposed changes because some might make things worse. So it seems wise to look at the current situation to see what is working well and merits conserving.

Perhaps an example will help. Imagine that a computer company proposed to give electronic tablets to all students in a school district. Company representatives say, *In today's world, it's never too soon to help children become sophisticated users of digital technology. By mastering this technology, children will become more independent learners and will be more competitive on the job market later in life. Digital platforms also allow teachers to use the newest methods to motivate students and help them learn at their own pace.* Perhaps this sounds plausible, even exciting, to many teachers and administrators. After all, isn't the latest technology the best? Doesn't it always produce better results? Well, then, it should of course be used in schools.

But note what is missing from the pitch for new technology: proof that it yields better results, consideration of its possible harmful effects on teachers and students, consideration of environmental costs, consideration of benefits offered by old technology (e.g., books), and skepticism about the ulterior motives of the company. Without taking these matters into account, it would be impossible to make a wise choice about whether to adopt the new technology. In a rush to embrace the new, we might end up abandoning good things that still work well.

The problem we always face is how to choose the best of the old and the best of the new. Sociology doesn't offer any formulas for doing this. Still, when we decide what to conserve and what to let go of, we can do it in a more sociologically mindful way, taking into account a wider range of potential consequences. This can improve our chances of conserving what is of value while also embracing change that is likely to make the world a better place. As I will suggest later, it can also improve the conversations we have about social change.

A Sociologically Mindful Approach to Conserving

I'm going to propose ways to think about the problem of what to conserve. Thinking along these lines doesn't lead to any particular conclusions. The point is to encourage a more thoughtful approach to conserving and, by implication, to change. Having a common set of considerations—things we all might want to take into account—can also foster more constructive dialogue about what to conserve and why. Here, then, are some suggestions about what to consider when faced with the problem of deciding what to conserve and what to try to change.

Consider who benefits and who pays. In the technology example (electronic tablets in schools) I used earlier, a promoter of the new technology might claim that its benefits outweigh its costs. But it's important to consider who pays the costs and who gets the benefits. It might be that, by some overall calculation, benefits outweigh costs; but if all the benefits go to one party and all the costs are borne by another, then the new technology is likely to create or amplify inequality. Perhaps existing technologies or practices produce an equal sharing of costs and benefits. If so, this might be a reason for conserving those technologies and practices, or for trying to more fairly distribute the costs and benefits of what's offered as new.

Consider external or hidden costs. This means looking for non-obvious costs. New computer technologies, for example, often impose environmental costs on places far from where the technologies are used. The environment elsewhere might be damaged by mining for metals, pollution from new factories, increased energy extraction, and disposal of old devices. Because these costs are usually unseen by consumers, it can take some researching to become aware of them. Taking these external or hidden costs into account, we might look for ways to conserve existing technologies or practices that impose fewer costs. At the very least, we will be skeptical about claims that a new technology or practice will yield only benefits and no costs.

Consider possible unintended consequences. The unintended consequences of change are hard to predict, but we can try to imagine, based on experience and research, what they might be. Electronic tablets, for example, might indeed make it easier for students to look up information, but they might also increase distraction in the classroom; discourage students from learning by making it seem that everything can be looked up online; disrupt nurturing relationships between teachers and students; and shift control of instruction from teachers to companies that care only about profits. If new technologies and practices seem likely to create these problems, then perhaps it would be better to stick with the old technologies and practices that don't.

Consider more than efficiency. Getting equally good or better results while expending less time, energy, effort, and money is generally desirable. But efficiency is not the only thing that makes society good and life worth living. We also value beauty, trust, solidarity, hope, compassion, neighborliness, and love—things that are hard to measure in terms of inputs and outputs. So we might ask, when considering new technologies and practices, how these other desirable features of human social life will be affected. If these less-tangible human goods are likely to be threatened by changes touted as "more efficient," we might reasonably resist those changes, or look for ways to ensure that we don't sacrifice many goods for a gain in only one.

Consider what is necessary to conserve and what is optional. We can live without rotary telephones, typewriters, and film cameras. We can live without playing football, eating hamburgers, and going to the movies. Even though many people enjoy these technologies and practices, none of them is essential to our survival. On the other hand, we can't live without breathable air and drinkable water. We can't live without fertile soil in which to grow crops. Many people would argue that we can't survive without the less-tangible goods mentioned in the previous paragraph. So when thinking about what to conserve, we should consider what is essential to our collective survival and what is not. If we don't conserve the former, all our considering will come to a foreshortened end.

Consider repair and restoration. Advertising encourages us to discard the old and replace it with the new, instead of thinking about how the old might be worth saving through repair or restoration. This throwaway attitude can affect our thinking not only about consumer goods but also about social arrangements. The result is a tendency to think about conserving in either/or terms—either we keep current arrangements as they are, or we replace them with something entirely new. Such thinking can lead people to take hardline positions, insisting on either no change or a complete overhaul. Neither position is realistic. What we might do instead is to consider how what now exists can be repaired or restored, if analysis reveals a need for fixing or improvement. Again, the goal is to hold on to what works and make it work better rather than try to reinvent the world from scratch.

Consider the lessons of the past. The knowledge we have conserved about the past can be used to guide our thinking about the future. What has happened in the past, we might ask, when societies failed to conserve democratic practices? What has happened when they failed to conserve civilian control of the military? What has happened when they failed to conserve the laws that protect citizens from government surveillance? What has happened when they failed to conserve the food or energy sources on which their material life depended? People will draw different lessons from the past, and apply those lessons differently to the present, but this is not a reason to ignore the past. Anything that might help us see what's at stake when we must decide what to conserve and what to change is worth a try.

The preceding considerations can be applied not only to changes in technology but also to changes in laws, policies, regulations, institutional practices, and cultural practices. When trying to assess the advisability of such changes, we can ask the same questions: Who will benefit and who will pay? What are the external or hidden costs? What are the possible unintended consequences? What is at stake besides efficiency? What is essential to conserve and what isn't? Is repair or restoration an option? And what can the past tell us about our current situation? Asking these questions and weighing the answers doesn't always prevent mistakes. All it ensures is more mindful participation in making history.

These same questions can be turned around and directed not only at proposed changes but also at the status quo. We can look at current laws, policies, and practices and ask, *Who benefits? Who pays? What are the costs?* and so on. Just as we can use these questions to think about what ought to be conserved, we can use them to think about what ought to be changed. If a few simple questions can do so much to help us rationally consider and discuss change, why is it still so hard to do this? Why does it cause so much conflict? The answer has to do with the struggle to conserve advantages in an unequal society.

Talking About What to Conserve

In highly unequal societies—those in which some people have far more wealth, status, and power than others—conversations about what to conserve are often fraught with fear and suspicion. People who currently enjoy advantages may fear, consciously or unconsciously, that change will deprive them of their advantages. People who seek change in pursuit of equality may suspect that every argument for conserving something masks a desire to retain power and privilege. These conditions make open and honest conversation difficult.

One partial solution to this problem is to organize conversations in ways that encourage analysis rather than argument. The considerations I put forth in the previous section can be used in this way. Each consideration can be the basis for a conversation about what to conserve and what to try to change. It is hard to hide ulterior motives and a desire to protect privilege if everyone agrees to use a set of analytic questions to better understand a situation. Too often, conversations about conserving and change go awry because the effort to develop understanding is bypassed as people rush to debate what's right or wrong to do.

Drawing on a set of ideas about what to discuss can put a conversation on track. But *how* we participate is equally important. Focusing on analytic questions makes it harder to mask the defense of power and privilege, harder to avoid facing problems that need to be solved—harder but not impossible. Much depends on whether we participate in good faith, with a genuine desire to reach mutual understanding, or as debaters desiring to win. The latter approach tends to submerge conflict, not resolve it. Here is what we can do to overcome this problem.

Reflect on our investments in the status quo. This means looking honestly at ourselves and asking why we want to conserve some law, policy, or practice. What's at stake for us? Perhaps what we're trying to conserve is not something that serves the common good, but something that serves mainly to make us feel virtuous, comfortable, or superior to others. If we aren't honest with ourselves about this, we might try hard to defend arrangements that we know, deep down, are causing others to suffer. And it's exactly this kind of unexamined defensiveness that can make conversation hard. If we reflect on our investments in the status quo, we can do a better job of balancing our interests in conserving against those of others who seek change. We can also put our conversational energy into seeking understanding and a way forward rather than into making self-serving arguments.

Listen and empathize. In conversations about what to conserve and what to change, listening (see chapter 2) and empathizing (see chapter 6) are essential. This is because people come to these conversations with strong feelings about what's right and wrong and about what should and shouldn't be changed. The stronger the feelings, the more likely it is that a conversation will fail if people don't listen and empathize. Doing these things doesn't mean giving up one's own feelings or beliefs, nor does it guarantee agreement. What listening and empathizing do is improve the chances of reaching mutual understanding, of seeing what's at stake for everyone, and of devising creative solutions to the problem of what to conserve and what to change.

Keep looking for common ground. People who embrace different political identities often really want the same things: safer, more neighborly communities; better educational and job opportunities for themselves and their children; more democratic and responsive government; affordable healthcare; a more equal distribution of wealth and power in society; and more mutual respect and fairness in everyday life. Ideally, conversations about change will reveal these common interests and shared values. But this is more likely to happen if there is intentional effort to find common ground, and so it's what we should keep looking for, even amidst seemingly intractable differences. Finding this common ground can in turn create an opening to discuss what to do next—how to conserve what is good and how to make the good better.

Everyone interested in creating a better world wants to conserve some things and change others. Which means that we all face our own version of the problem of how to decide what to conserve and what to try to change. But of course we are not in this alone. As members of groups and communities, we must also negotiate competing, sometimes strongly conflicting, interests in conserving and changing different parts of the social world. The suggestions I've offered can perhaps help us do this with less strife. By taking a more mindful approach to conserving, we increase the chances of having the kind of conversations that make peaceful change possible.

To Learn More

Abbey, Edward. (1991). *Down the River.* New York: Plume.
Berry, Wendell. (1990). *What Are People For?* San Francisco: North Point Press.
Berry, Wendell. (2003). *Citizenship Papers.* Washington, DC: Shoemaker & Hoard.
Etzioni, Amitai. (2004). *The Common Good.* New York: Polity.
Genette, John, Linde, Jennifer, and Olson, Clark D. (2017). *Hot Topics, Cool Heads: A Handbook for Civil Dialogue.* Dubuque, IA: Kendall Hunt Publishing.
Goleman, Daniel, Bennett, Lisa, and Barlow, Zenobia. (2012). *Eco Literate.* New York: Jossey-Bass.
Goodall, Jane. (2000). *Reason for Hope* (revised ed.). New York: Grand Central Publishing.

Levitsky, Steven, and Ziblatt, Daniel. (2018). *How Democracies Die*. New York: Crown.

Oliver, Mary. (2016). *Upstream*. New York: Penguin.

Reich, Robert B. (2018). *The Common Good*. New York: Knopf.

Snyder, Gary. (2010). *The Practice of the Wild* (expanded ed.). Berkeley, CA: Counterpoint.

Spelman, Elizabeth V. (2002). *Repair: The Impulse to Restore in a Fragile World*. Boston: Beacon.

Vitek, Bill, and Jackson, Wes (eds.). (2010). *The Virtues of Ignorance: Complexity, Sustainability, and the Limits of Knowledge*. Lexington, KY: University of Kentucky Press.

CHAPTER 9

Teaching

The title of this chapter might lead some readers to think, "I'll skip this one, because I don't want to be a teacher." But please don't leave yet. I'm *not* going to say that everyone should pursue a career as a teacher. I'm going to say that everyone who is trying to make a difference can't help being a teacher, and that teaching others is a natural part of trying to make a difference. We often fail to see this because much of the teaching I'm referring to doesn't happen in a classroom.

Of course I'm not discounting classroom teaching or teaching as a career. Teaching is a noble calling and one of the best ways to help change others' lives for the better. It would be a good thing, I think, if more people became teachers. But it's not possible for everyone to earn a living as a teacher. Nor is it necessary to make a living as a teacher to teach in a way that can help make the world a better place.

When I say that everyone trying to make a difference can't help being a teacher, I mean that we all teach by example. No matter what we say or do, there is always some audience that will take a lesson from it. If we speak out against injustice or we try to change the conditions that cause others to suffer, we show that apathy and resignation are not the only options. If we do nothing, our inaction might convey the lesson that nothing much needs to be changed.

When I say that teaching others is a natural part of trying to make a difference, I mean that part of what produces social change is transmitting ideas, knowledge, and skills to others. When we do these things, in the course of working for change, we act as teachers, whether we call ourselves teachers or not. All the practices I've described in this book—listening, writing, organizing, empathizing, advocating, researching, and conserving—must be learned. Once learned, they can be taught to others, and by so doing, we amplify our power to make change.

So my goal is not to convince people to go into teaching as a career; rather, I want to encourage a view of teaching as a practice that is essential for creating a better world. Seen in this way, teaching is more than just a way someone might try to make a living. It is part of living in a way that can make a positive difference. And like the other practices I've described, it is something we can learn to do in more sociologically mindful and effective ways.

Much of what I said in chapter 4 about writing was no doubt familiar to experienced writers. Likewise, much of what I have to say about teaching will be familiar to experienced teachers. I make no claims to secret knowledge or hitherto unknown ideas about how to teach. Yet what is already well known is not necessarily widely known, so perhaps what I have to say, if it seems obvious to some, will be new to others. What might also be new and helpful, I hope, is consideration of how sociological mindfulness can enhance the teaching we do in pursuit of social change.

Sociologically Mindful Teaching

All intentional teaching requires awareness of the need to make instruction sensible to a learner who sees the world from another perspective. Any teacher who understands this is already being sociologically mindful. But there is more to it. Sociologically mindful teaching involves paying attention to how interaction, context, diversity, and inequality affect learning. The point is not just to "pay attention" to these matters but to change how one acts as a teacher. Below I propose some practices that follow from taking a sociologically mindful approach to teaching—in the classroom, in social movement organizations, or in everyday life.

Start where learners are. It doesn't make sense to teach people things they already know. Nor does it make sense to jump ahead and try to teach people things that they don't have a foundation for learning. When I teach a sociology course, I know where to start because I know which prerequisites students have met. When I teach a nonacademic course—about, say, photography—I begin by finding out how much people already know and what they want to learn. If I didn't do this, I could end up wasting everyone's time.

Still, it's often hard to "start where learners are" when teaching a class. This is because people in classes—even if they've met the same prerequisites, are about the same age, and claim to have similar backgrounds—are always different. Some people know more than others, some are more ready to learn, some are quicker to learn, some are more determined to learn. Which means that all learners in a class are never in precisely the same place. You've probably seen this for yourself. It's a problem built in to how most schools are organized.

It is easier to figure out where to begin with one learner, outside of a classroom. Through talk and demonstration (as in, "show me what you can do"), a teacher, mentor, or master craftsperson can determine how much a student, mentee, or apprentice knows and what s/he can do. The proper starting point is then one step beyond where the learner is at. Being mindful of the starting point problem helps to avoid teaching that is boring because it repeats what a learner already knows, or frustrating because it presumes too much.

Link learning to doing. I could teach you that Bismarck is the capital of North Dakota without asking you to go there and verify it for yourself (in fact, you've just learned this, with no more action involved than reading a sentence). But if I were going to teach you to ride a bicycle, use a welding torch, or play baseball, it would be impossible to do so without physical action. I would have to demonstrate and you'd have to give it a try; verbal explanation wouldn't be enough. So in some cases, it's obvious that teaching and learning must be linked to doing.

In other cases, it's less obvious. Take the example of learning that Bismarck is the capital of North Dakota. I could just tell you this, and you might remember it (if it was important for some reason). But if I asked you—imagine that I'm your 5th-grade geography teacher—to write and deliver a report on the history, culture, politics, and economy of North Dakota, you'd learn a lot more. Including that Bismarck is the capital city. This is a way to link learning to doing, even when what needs to be taught and learned consists of ideas and information rather than manual skills.

Linking learning to doing reflects awareness that people learn in different ways. When it comes to riding a bicycle, everybody has to learn by doing. With other things, learning styles can vary, based on people's prior experiences; some people thrive on verbal instruction, others need more doing. Good teachers figure out what works best for a particular learner. Again, this is harder to do in classes than in one-on-one instruction. Which may be why many people, especially adults, learn more from mentors than from teachers in school.

Praise the good. When trying to acquire complex ideas and information, it's common to get things wrong at first. When trying to acquire new skills, it's common to make mistakes. Yes, some people learn more quickly than others, but no one is faultless from the start. This means that learners need correction, and it befalls teachers to do the correcting. In fact, this seems to be what a lot of teaching in schools amounts to: telling students what they did wrong and hoping that they'll do better the next time.

Correcting mistakes is not necessarily a bad form of feedback. Sometimes it's what's needed, though much depends on how it's delivered: in a gentle and nurturing way, or a harsh way. Gentle and nurturing is almost always better, presuming that the message—about what needs improvement—gets through. But a steady stream of negative feedback, absent the positive, can be discouraging. Oftentimes a better method is to downplay mistakes, or ignore them entirely, and focus on what is done correctly and well.

Praising the good works because it builds the confidence necessary to persevere when learning is hard. It also tells learners what they should aim for, and this leads learners to put more effort into doing what's right and stop doing what isn't. Another reason that praising the good works has to do with inequalities between teachers and learners. Because teachers have more power in the relationship, and often have higher status, learners usually look up to their teachers and want to please them. Showing students what to do to earn approval can thus nurture both skills and motivation.

Ask questions. There is an old saying that what keeps us from learning is what we think we already know. After all, if the knowledge we possess is adequate and correct, why bother to learn more? It will just require time and energy and leave us no better off. Here is where teachers can productively disrupt complacency. One way teachers do this is by asking questions.

By asking the right questions, teachers can help learners see the limits of their knowledge. Teaching by questioning is easy to imagine in sports and games. For example, a baseball coach might ask, If there is one out, a runner at first, and the batter hits a ground ball to short, where is the play? A chess coach might ask, If white opens with the Ruy Lopez, what is black's best defense? Other kinds of teachers can do the same sort of thing. A research methods teacher might ask, When is it better to use a stratified random sample rather than a simple random sample? By asking these kinds of questions, a teacher helps a learner develop foresight and the ability to solve problems.

Teachers can also ask questions to expose beliefs that impede learning. For example, students who believe that in America anyone can get ahead if they just work hard and play by the rules often struggle to see how social structure makes inequality inevitable. So I ask, If everyone in US society were smart, ambitious, hard working, law abiding, and so forth, would everyone get a great, high-paying job? Most students recognize that the answer is no because there aren't enough great, high-paying jobs; most people would still end up in mediocre or lousy jobs. So by asking a simple question, it's possible to reveal a false belief that gets in the way of learning an important lesson about how inequality is reproduced in US society.

Teach learning. We usually think of teachers as transmitting "content" of some kind: facts, concepts, skills. This is a reasonable way to think about what teaching can accomplish. But there is something else that teaching always teaches, if only inadvertently: how to learn. Whatever method a teacher uses—lecturing, demonstrating, discussing, assigning readings, giving feedback on learners' performances—conveys messages about how learning can and should be done. Sometimes these messages are more valuable than the manifest content.

There is a useful body of knowledge about how people achieve mastery in a field (see To Learn More at the end of the chapter). Practice is important, but it must be what is called "deliberate practice." This entails working on the right skills at the right time, stretching a little beyond one's current limits, a lot of repetition, and continuous feedback to refine technique. Good teachers create this kind of regimen for learners. Here again, teaching one-on-one offers the advantage of being able to get to know a learner and discern exactly what that learner needs to do to improve.

A teacher who can help a learner engage in deliberate practice might be wonderfully effective. The risk is that this process can make a learner dependent on a teacher. Long-term learning is thus better fostered by teaching learners how to teach themselves. Sometimes this means teaching the components of deliberate practice—identifying and overcoming weaknesses, pushing beyond one's current limits, repetition, seeking and using feedback—and sometimes it means teaching a method of inquiry (i.e., how to find and evaluate information). Either way, by teaching learning, teachers can empower others to learn and grow over a lifetime, long after a class or set of lessons is over.

Teach by example. Earlier I said that part of living as a teacher is being aware that we are always teaching by example, if only because others take lessons from watching what we do. Being aware of this, we can try to live so as to convey more positive lessons than cautionary ones. Although this might seem like the most passive form of teaching, it can be quite powerful. If I say, "You should drive with both hands on the steering wheel at all times," but then you see me use only the fingers of one hand, what lesson are you likely to take?

Here is another example:

Suppose I wanted to write about teaching as a way to make the world a better place. I could jot down some ideas off the top of my head and start dashing off sentences. If you saw me do this, you might suppose that the way to write a book is to ignore the wisdom of others and jump right in. But that would be a faulty lesson. So here is the truth: even though I've been teaching for a long time, before I wrote this chapter I read or reread half a dozen books about teaching. I did this to refresh my memory and look for new ideas. What is the lesson in this? That no matter how much you think you know, it's good to stay in touch with the thoughts of others.

Here is one more example:

Suppose I wrote the following sentence: *Writing for the general public and other nonacademic audiences is a worthwhile thing to do because it's a way to try to make the world a better place by sharing ideas and information and analysis with other people who might benefit from finding out what you have to say about social problems and what causes them and what might be some possible solutions.* That's not the worst sentence in the world (at least it makes sense), but it's ponderous and dull; no one would want to read a book full of such sentences. So it needs to be tightened and sharpened, possibly like this: *Public writing can make the world a better place by helping people understand social problems and how to solve them.* That's not the best sentence in the world, but it's better, and it took a while to figure out—just like all the sentences in this book. If this example of how writing is improved by revision gets the point across, then I've also made a point about the power of teaching by example.

Stress work, not talent. We often talk about teachers, coaches, and mentors "spotting talent" and nurturing it. If talent were always understood to mean potential, then this would be a reasonable way to talk. But talent is usually taken to mean an innate quality or mysterious essence—something naturally inside a person—that produces excellence. When it comes to teaching, this is a pernicious notion. It does more harm than good.

There are at least two problems with the notion of talent. One is that it creates the impression that some people, those who have the requisite talent, can learn to excel; and others, those who lack talent, can't. This idea leads many people, often those from less-privileged groups, to think that there is no point in trying to learn X or in striving to be excellent at X because they don't have the talent for it. The other problem is that the idea of talent masks what really produces learning and excellence: the right kinds of actions—often involving a tremendous amount of work—on the part of teachers and learners.

Part of mindful teaching is getting learners to undertake the right kinds of actions (see above about deliberate practice). What good teachers, coaches, and mentors also know, from their own experience, are the component techniques that go into producing excellence. These are, as it is sometimes said, "all the little things" that must be done right to excel in a sport, an occupation, a craft, or other challenging activity. Good teachers not only know what these things are, they also nurture the discipline and attitudes that make learners willing to try, again and again, to do all the little things right. It's this kind of determined effort that leads to excellence. The notion of talent just gets in the way by making excellence seem to be the result of natural gifts rather than, more mundanely, the result of an understandable social process that mindful teachers can use to develop learners' potential, whatever that potential might be.

Living as Teachers

Even though we can't all make a living as teachers, we can all try to live as teachers. This doesn't mean subjecting people to uninvited lectures. It means, first, caring about the growth and learning of others, both children and adults, and being aware of the need to provide opportunities for them to grow and learn. Are we doing enough to ensure that every child and every adult has the resources and support they need to learn? Are we doing it well enough? To ask these questions is to begin living as a teacher.

Living as a teacher also means living with awareness that we always teach by example. As I said earlier, no matter what we say or do, someone will take a lesson from it. Being aware of this shouldn't make us neurotic, as if we must constantly strive for sainthood; all we can do is the best we can, given the circumstances we face. But if we pay attention to our power to teach by example, we realize that we have many opportunities to add to the growth and learning of others. To live as a teacher is to teach by how one lives.

Living as a teacher also means being concerned with how we organize ourselves to transmit knowledge and skills, and to preserve collective memory, not just in schools but throughout society. What kinds of libraries, museums, and memorials do we create? How do we ensure that knowledge is preserved and made available to all? These are questions that implicate collective action—how we work together to create organizations and institutions that will teach new generations. Being part of this process, advocating for education and for the right to education, is part of living as a teacher.

What I am urging is not just awareness of the importance of teaching and learning, but taking responsibility for making these things happen. If more knowledge is better than less knowledge, if more understanding is better than less understanding, then anything we can do to promote these social goods helps to make the world a better place. Sometimes we can do this directly, by interacting with others as teachers, tutors, coaches, and mentors. Sometimes we can do it only indirectly, by supporting others' efforts to teach. Either way, we can meet some part of a shared responsibility to aid the growth and learning of others.

Some readers might be impatient with this notion of living as a teacher. Perhaps it seems insufficiently vigorous as a way to pursue change. After all, there is nothing especially radical about "advocating for education." Even people in power, those who benefit greatly from the status quo and want to keep it from changing, speak about the value of education. Skeptics might also say that schooling does more to slot people into the status quo than it does to equip them to challenge and change it.

I appreciate this critique of *schooling*. But my concern is *education*, and much depends, I would say, on what kind of education, about what, is being advocated for whom. One might, for example, call for better education about injustices inflicted on subordinated groups; or for more education about the damage caused by concentrated wealth and power; or for more attention to knowledge and skills needed to pursue change. As I noted in chapter 5 on organizing, teaching about US labor history and other social movements could convey important lessons about the need for dissent (see chapter 10), collective action, and solidarity to make change.

In the end, it is probably less important what happens in conventional schools than what happens in workshops, mentoring relationships, social movement organizations, training programs for organizers, and informal conversations. It is in these contexts that the knowledge and skills helpful for making change are most likely to be imparted, free from demands to reproduce class and status hierarchies. The tips I offered earlier can help make this teaching—teaching explicitly aimed at social change—more effective. If we can also do it in a sociologically mindful way, it can make even more of a difference.

To Learn More

Atkinson, Maxine, and Lowney, Kathleen S. (2014). *In the Trenches: Teaching and Learning Sociology*. New York: W. W. Norton & Company.

Chambliss, Daniel. (1989). "The Mundanity of Excellence: An Ethnographic Report on Stratification and Olympic Swimmers." *Sociological Theory* 7(1): 70–86.

Chambliss, Daniel, and Takacs, Christopher G. (2014). *How College Works*. Cambridge, MA: Harvard University Press.

Colvin, Geoff. (2010). *Talent is Overrated: What Really Separates World-Class Performers from Everybody Else*. New York: Penguin.

Duncan-Andrade, Jeffrey M. (2008). *The Art of Critical Pedagogy: Possibilities for Moving from Theory to Practice in Urban Schools*. New York: Peter Lang.

Ericsson, Anders, and Pool, Robert. (2016). *Peak: Secrets from the New Science of Expertise*. Boston: Eamon Dolan/Houghton Mifflin Harcourt.

Freire, Paulo. (2018). *Pedagogy of the Oppressed* (50th anniversary ed.). New York: Bloomsbury.

Hooks, Bell. (1994). *Teaching to Transgress: Education as the Practice of Freedom*. New York: Routledge.

Mali, Taylor. (2012). *What Teachers Make: In Praise of the Greatest Job in the World*. New York: Berkley Books.

Noddings, Nel, and Brooks, Laurie. (2016). *Teaching Controversial Issues: The Case for Critical Thinking and Moral Commitment in the Classroom*. New York: Teachers College Press.

Postman, Neil, and Weingartner, Charles. (1969). *Teaching as a Subversive Activity*. New York: Delta/Dell.

Shor, Ira. (1980). *Critical Teaching and Everyday Life*. Boston: South End Press.

Shor, Ira. (1992). *Empowering Education: Critical Teaching for Social Change*. Chicago: University of Chicago Press.

CHAPTER 10

....

Dissenting

I f I had been more experienced, I probably would have found a different way to deal with Robert. I was teaching a social problems course, not long after I got my PhD, and Robert (as I'll call him here) found something to disagree with during every class. At first I thought he was just an enthusiastic and curious student who wanted to learn more. I had invited dialogue about anything related to the course, so I couldn't very well complain if Robert took me up on the offer.

But after a while I began to worry about how much time it was taking to respond to Robert's frequent and sometimes picayune objections. I also began to wonder about his sincerity. My doubts were confirmed one day when I overheard Robert and another student talking in the hallway before class. "You must really dislike Professor Schwalbe," his classmate said. "Nah," Robert said, "he's okay. I just like to give him a hard time to bug his ass." I was disappointed to hear that, but it gave me an idea.

At that point in the semester we were covering environmental issues. So at the start of the next class, I said that I wanted to take a few minutes to discuss the recent Supreme Court decision in the case of *Ourea v. Acheron Coal Company*. I said that what the Court had decided, in a nutshell, was that people could sue the coal company for the harm that mountaintop removal would inflict on future generations. I said that local landowners and environmentalists had hailed the decision as a victory for their side. Then I paused and said, "But surely Robert will have some contrary thoughts about this." He did.

Robert described the decision as an instance of activist judges making up laws that would hurt business and destroy jobs in the coal industry. He also said that there was no possible way to assess costs to future generations. I was glad to hear him speak with authority. When he finished, I said, "That's an interesting opinion, especially since there is no such case as *Ourea v. Acheron Coal Company.* I just made it up." There was silence in the room. Some students looked at Robert, some looked at me. Then Robert said, "Well, I thought you were talking about a different case." With that, I let him off the hook.

My prank had the intended effect on Robert's behavior. After that class, he began to ask better questions and make more thoughtful comments. I had made my point about the importance—if we were going to discuss social problems in a serious, analytic way—of knowing what one is talking about and not just being a gadfly. Yes, tricking Robert was a little mean, and I never did that sort of thing again (at least not to an individual student). I tell the story here, at some risk of embarrassment, because it's useful for distinguishing between contrarianism and dissent.

Robert's behavior is an example of contrarianism—objecting for the sake of standing out as a rebel. "I am such a bold and unbridled thinker," the contrarian seems to say, "that I will reject dominant views no matter what they are or where I confront them." Being skeptical of dominant views is a good thing, as I have been saying all along. On the other hand, this can be taken to silly extremes ("The earth is flat!"); it can be obstructive if it is impervious to fact; and it can be destructive if it impedes honest dialogue.

Dissent is different. To dissent is to refuse to accept the views and practices preferred by those in power. It is to refuse to conform or obey—intellectually, behaviorally, or in both ways. But dissent is not knee-jerk rejection of authority. It's carefully considered action undertaken because the dissenter sincerely believes that dominant views and practices are morally wrong, based on bad information or faulty arguments, or likely to be destructive. And whereas a contrarian seeks the notoriety of being a rebel, a dissenter seeks to make a group, organization, community, or society work better.

Dissent can take many forms: asking questions, injecting new information or perspectives into a conversation, raising objections, condemning harmful ideas or practices, whistle-blowing to expose corruption, withholding cooperation (i.e., refusing to obey), and organizing resistance to the status quo. These can all be thought of as forms of troublemaking, if "trouble" is defined as any refusal to quietly accept the dictates of the powerful or to go along with business as usual. But, again, the purpose of dissent is not to cause trouble but to spur constructive change.

Most people are not dissenters. Out of fear of disapproval or other punishment, most people conform and obey. As it is sometimes said, most people "take the path of least resistance." This is the path that keeps the social world operating in the same old ways. But hard though it might be, dissent is always a possibility; the choice to dissent is always ours. We can decide, despite the short-term costs, to dissent in measured, strategic ways, keeping in mind the long-term goal of making the world a better place.

The Social Value of Dissent

How can refusing to think or act in ways expected by those in power make the world a better place? It depends, of course, on what one is dissenting from and advocating for. As with all the practices discussed in this book, dissent can be undertaken to promote equality, fairness, democracy, and peace—or not. But here I want to set aside this (ever-present) concern and make a case for the value of dissent in general. My claim is that dissent, though it might trouble some people, is essential to social well-being. Here is why.

Dissent enhances creativity. Taking the path of least resistance keeps the social world operating in the same old ways. This might also be called thinking and acting "inside the box"—that is, in safe and familiar ways. If everyone did this all the time, there would be no new ideas or new ways of doing things. Groups, organizations, and communities would stagnate. So where do new ideas come from? How does it occur to us to do things differently? Dissent is the key. By challenging conventional or dominant views, dissenters can force a re-evaluation of the old ways and spark conversations about change. Dissent, in other words, is what gets us thinking outside the box.

Dissent improves democratic decision-making. In democratic groups and communities, decisions are supposed to be made by sharing information and ideas, discussing options, and seeking workable agreement about what to do. But what if someone who has potentially useful information and ideas holds back—fails to speak up—because everyone else seems to think differently? This means that the best decision might not be reached because a vital piece of input is missing. In such a case, dissenting from what seems like the dominant view can lead to more informed, thoughtful, and creative decision-making. Dissent can thus benefit a group, organization, or community because it means that more information and ideas are brought to bear on solving shared problems.

Dissent can overcome pluralistic ignorance. Suppose that many people in a group (or organization or community) dislike how the group is governed. Perhaps decisions are made by self-serving elites, with no democratic checks and balances. But also suppose that no one speaks up to object. It will appear that everyone thinks things are okay. This is a situation of pluralistic ignorance—people don't know what others are thinking and feeling. In these cases, dissent can break the spell. When one dissenter speaks up, others realize that they are not alone and begin to speak up too. Sometimes this sparks new conversations, thoughts, and organizing efforts (see chapter 5) about what needs to be done to solve the problems that people now see that they share.

Dissent can expose corruption. What is to stop people who wield governmental or economic power from using that power for selfish gains? What is to stop them from doing things that are illegal, immoral, or harmful to others? Laws, regulatory policies, and democratic oversight are supposed to serve as safeguards. But these safeguards are often thwarted by secrecy. This is why so-called whistle-blowers are important. Whistle-blowers dissent by refusing to maintain the secrecy that allows powerful people to act without accountability. By exposing dishonest, corrupt, and incompetent practices—exposing these practices so that they can be stopped or changed—whistle-blowing can make groups, organizations, and communities better serve the common good.

Dissent can deter crimes of obedience. Crimes of obedience are crimes committed by people who are doing what they think their bosses (or other leaders) expect of them. When called to account, perpetrators often say, "I was just following orders." Civilian massacres during wartime are perhaps the most dramatic and familiar examples. But crimes of obedience can occur wherever people feel compelled to follow orders to keep their jobs or avoid punishment. In such cases, a single dissenter—one person who speaks up and refuses to engage in illegal or immoral behavior—can make a difference because the act of dissent helps others see that what is being demanded by those in power is wrong. One person dissenting also shatters the illusion that everyone agrees it's okay to do what those in power want. Sometimes a single act of resistance will spark wider dissent and prevent a crime of obedience from happening.

Dissent can serve the future. Acts of dissent might not persuade others to think or behave differently in an immediate situation. People might feel too powerfully compelled to conform and obey. This can make it seem that dissent is pointless. But sometimes the information and ideas put forward by a dissenter need time to germinate. People might take in a dissenter's arguments but not yet be willing to act differently. Later, when conditions are ripe, those arguments might gain new traction. So while it might seem that dissent is making no difference now, it can make a difference later. If dissent does not change the world today, it might still make for a better future.

What I have been pointing to here are the benefits that groups, organizations, and communities can derive from dissent. Where dissent is present, there is likely to be more innovation, better "public reasoning" and democratic decision-making, less pluralistic ignorance (or more mutual understanding), less corruption, fewer crimes of obedience, and better prospects for peaceful change. Later I'll suggest how we can create conditions that foster constructive dissent. But first I want to offer some suggestions for how anyone who wants to make the world a better place can dissent more effectively.

Mindful Dissent

If dissent is defined as refusing to accept the status quo and trying to make the world a better place, then all the previous chapters and all the suggestions I've made (about what to do) are relevant to dissenting.

Listening, organizing, writing, teaching, researching, empathizing, and advocating are all potentially ways to dissent, or parts of the process of dissenting. Even conserving, when it means resisting destruction of the good, can be a form of dissent.

But here I've been discussing dissent as explicit objection to dominant, taken-for-granted ideas and practices—objection that can involve refusal to conform, obey, and cooperate, especially when demands come from those in power. Dissent, when it is this forthright, is tricky. Dissenters risk being seen as mere troublemakers; they risk disapproval—not only by those in power but also by peers and potential allies. There are, however, ways to reduce these risks and make dissent more effective. Here is what I suggest.

Clarify the reasons for dissent. What is it about current conditions, rules, or demands that is intolerable? Which facts, values, or principles are being ignored or dismissed? Why do these facts, values, or principles matter? Which desirable outcomes are threatened? Reflecting on these questions is necessary to figure out how to justify and explain dissent. If we can clarify what's at stake, we can do a better job of presenting information and ideas to others. It's also important to examine our motives because authenticity matters too. Dissent is more persuasive when it is seen as arising from true beliefs and convictions rather than from a desire to pose as a rebel. This is why people who are contrary for the sake of being contrary are rarely effective as dissenters.

Muster evidence and arguments. It's possible to dissent by saying, "I just feel that X is wrong, so I won't go along with it." In some cases, this might be what one has to say. On the other hand, by itself, this is unlikely to sway others who are ready to conform and obey, perhaps because they have already decided that X is okay. What's more persuasive is to be able to explain, in terms that others will understand, why X is wrong. What values does it offend? What harm does it (or will it) cause? How can we know this? By making arguments, rather than just declarations, others are more likely to see dissent as legitimate and be willing to give it a hearing. Making arguments is also more likely to prompt constructive conversation about alternative courses of action. To just declare that X is wrong doesn't do much to help others see what to do differently. So, in addition to presenting evidence and arguments, it is also wise for dissenters to present concrete alternatives to what is objectionable.

Talk, listen, and organize first. We often picture a dissenter as a person who stands alone against something that person sees as wrong. Sometimes this image fits reality. But perhaps more often, especially in the case of social movements, dissenters talk to others, listen to others, and coordinate with others before their dissent becomes visible. There are good reasons for doing this. One is to check one's own perceptions of a situation against those of others. Another is to find out why others are inclined not to dissent. A further reason is to connect with others who are sympathetic. Finding out how others think can help in formulating arguments that others will find reasonable rather than crazy. Finding out how others think is also a way to identify allies and begin organizing a campaign of dissent that can go beyond making individual statements.

Speak to common values and interests. Dissenters risk being seen as disloyal. "Who is this person," others might think, "to question how we have always done things? Who is this person to challenge the rightful authorities? Perhaps this person is not really one of us!" Dissenters who speak only of their individual values or interests affirm this perception and thus often fail to win support. But by speaking to the shared values and interests of a group, organization, or community, a dissenter has a better chance of being heard. Of course, this might not always be possible; a dissenter might fundamentally oppose the values and interests of a group, in which case there is no shared ground. Still, I would advise looking for shared ground (see chapter 6 on empathizing) before presuming that it does not exist. If dissent can be framed as serving the common good, it is more likely to make a difference.

Use humor. Humor is a partial antidote to the fear that compels people to conform and obey. If people can be made to see the absurdity of a situation and laugh about it, they might be more willing to listen to a dissenting argument. Likewise, if the authorities who demand conformity and obedience can be satirized, mocked, or ridiculed, their fearsomeness is diminished. Humor also makes an organized campaign of dissent more attractive to fence sitters. People who might be put off by a campaign that seems dark and dour might be attracted by one that encourages laughter—even while pursuing serious goals. The trick to using humor is to channel the energy it releases back into working for change rather than letting it serve only as a way to blow off steam.

Dissent to build democracy. Conformity, obedience, and the unreflective acceptance of dominant views are the opposites of democracy. If democracy means anything, it means working with fellow citizens to analyze problems, discuss solutions, and struggle toward agreement about what to do. As I said earlier, dissent is essential to this process; without it, we remain stuck in pedestrian thinking. I suggest keeping this idea in mind as a way to gain support for dissent. If dissenting is explained to others as part of the democratic process—as necessary to keep as many people as possible engaged in finding solutions to shared problems—it is more likely to be welcomed than to be disparaged as troublemaking. Organized campaigns of dissent (or "protest movements") are also opportunities to practice democracy and thereby create an example of what a more democratic society would look like.

Escalate gradually. Dissent can be mild and polite, loud and disruptive, or somewhere in between. One reason for starting off mild and polite is that it might work, and no greater effort will be needed. Another reason is that sudden disruption is likely to alarm potential supporters and make the orderly status quo seem attractive. Disruption that people don't yet understand—*What is this protest about? What is the problem? Why are these people making such a fuss?*—also tends to heighten fear of change. To be effective, dissent must be accompanied by education that makes a case for its necessity (see chapter 9 on teaching).

If mild and polite dissent—letters, petitions—is ignored by authorities, as it often is, then more assertive tactics—rallies, marches—gain legitimacy. If these more assertive tactics are still ignored, then disruptive tactics—strikes, sit-ins, civil disobedience—may be seen as warranted, provided that dissenters clearly explain these actions. Carefully measured escalation also signals determination. It sends a message to those in power that dissent is not going away, and that the costs of ignoring dissent will rise until change is made.

Making Constructive Dissent Possible

If we think of dissent as arising out of a clash between individual conscience and the demands of authority, then dissent would seem to depend mainly on courage. Perhaps a degree of courage is always needed, given the risks that dissent can entail. But like any other kind of social behavior, dissent depends on culture, context, and interaction, not just personality. This suggests that dissent can be fostered or impeded by social conditions. If we recognize the value of dissent, we might want to consider what these conditions are and how to create them.

I have already alluded to one such condition: belief in the value of dissent. If people in a group, organization, or community see dissent as a threat that must be quashed, then it's less likely to occur than if people see it as promoting creativity, better decision-making, and wider participation (rather than silence or withdrawal). Dissent is also more likely if people see it as a practice that helps root out corruption and deter crimes of obedience. We can encourage these understandings by speaking, writing, and teaching about the value of dissent, before and after it arises.

We can go further and make laws that protect dissenters. There are, for example, laws in some places that protect whistle-blowers from retaliation by their bosses. Laws that require openness in government decision-making can also encourage dissent by exposing actions that many people might oppose. Laws and organizational policies (e.g., tenure) that require due process before people can be fired from their jobs can also protect dissenters and encourage people to speak up, even in the face of power. Strengthening such laws and policies is a way to create conditions conducive to dissent.

In the United States, an important law for enabling dissent is the First Amendment to the Constitution. This part of the Bill of Rights grants us the freedom to speak our minds on public issues, associate with others as we wish, and publish information and opinions without government interference. It protects dissenters from being stifled by bosses and politicians who might prefer tyranny to democracy. But the First Amendment itself must be protected. Understanding its value and defending its use, even if we don't always like how it is used, are crucial for maintaining conditions that make dissent possible. The alternative is to let those in power decide what can and cannot be said.

In chapter 7, I said that advocating often takes the form of people in powerful groups speaking in support of people in less powerful groups. Another form it can take is trying to ensure that dissenting views get a fair hearing. In the end, those views might be rejected. But if they are at least allowed to be heard, it is less likely that those who hold them will feel disrespected and decide to withdraw from or sabotage the group, organization, or community. Simply making room for dissent doesn't ensure that conflicts and schisms will be avoided. But trying to quash dissent almost always worsens conflict, even if it appears to be submerged for a time.

Belief in the value of dissent, laws and policies that protect dissenters, and the practices of inviting and considering dissenting views make constructive dissent more likely. Promoting these beliefs and practices helps to ensure that the groups, organizations, and communities to which we belong do not become stagnant, corrupt, or authoritarian. Even when we do not feel compelled to dissent ourselves, we can be mindful of the need to create and maintain the conditions that make it possible.

The German writer Johann Goethe said that the world can be brought forward only by those who oppose it. This aphorism captures an important sociological insight: to create a social world in which there is more equality, fairness, democracy, and peace requires objecting to the beliefs and practices that now produce inequality, injustice, tyranny, and violence. Change, in other words, requires disruption. By dissenting in a sociologically mindful way, we are more likely to disrupt the status quo constructively, bringing the world forward and helping to make it a better place.

To Learn More

Brownlee, Kimberley. (2012). *Conscience and Conviction: The Case for Civil Disobedience*. New York: Oxford University Press.

Gamson, William, A. (1990). *The Strategy of Social Protest* (2nd ed.). Belmont, CA: Wadsworth Publishing.

Greenwald, Glenn. (2015). *No Place to Hide: Edward Snowden, the NSA, and the U.S. Surveillance State*. New York: Picador.

Hsaio, Andrew, and Lim, Audrea (eds.). (2010). *The Verso Book of Dissent: From Spartacus to the Shoe-Thrower of Baghdad*. London: Verso.

Jetten, Jolanda, and Hornsey, Matthew, J. (eds.). (2011). *Rebels in Groups: Dissent, Deviance, Difference and Defiance*. Chichester, UK: Wiley-Blackwell.

Piven, Frances F. (2006). *Challenging Authority: How Ordinary People Change America*. Lanham, MD: Rowman & Littlefield.

Popovic, Srdja. (2015). *Blueprint for Revolution*. New York: Spiegel & Grau.

Sharp, Gene. (2002). *From Dictatorship to Democracy*. New York: The New Press.

Sunstein, Cass. (2003). *Why Societies Need Dissent*. Cambridge, MA: Harvard University Press.

Young, Ralph. (2015). *Dissent: The History of an American Idea*. New York: New York University Press.

Zinn, Howard. (1968). *Disobedience and Democracy: Nine Fallacies on Law and Order*. New York: Random House.

CHAPTER 11

....

Imagining

A few years ago, I imagined writing a book in which I would explain how to work for change in a sociologically mindful way. I tried to imagine what I would say, dropping notes into a file as ideas occurred to me. At some point, when I was done with other projects, I had to imagine how I would start writing this new book, perhaps to be called *Making a Difference*. I had to think of a first sentence, a second sentence, and so on. If you are holding such a book in your hands, then it seems that my imagining has come to some sort of fruition.

The process I'm describing is both ordinary and special. It's ordinary in the sense that everyone who makes something goes through a similar process. The thing to be made—a book, a business, a garden, a meal—must be imagined before it can be brought into existence. What will eventually become a tangible reality first exists only in mind. Once we have at a least a rough mental blueprint, we can begin using our hands, tools, and materials to start crafting the thing we want to create.

What's special about this process is that only humans can do it, and it gives us great power to shape the world. We know that other animals can use rocks and sticks to get at food, so tool use is not uniquely human. But what humans alone can do is to imagine complex objects that don't exist in nature and then create those objects. Unlike animals that are biologically programmed to build particular things (e.g., nests, hives, dams) in particular ways, humans can imagine and build almost anything. We are, as it is sometimes said, "universal builders." One time I was asked to give a talk to a group of honors students who were majoring in engineering. I thought they might be stick-in-the-mud types, their minds fixed solely on practicalities in the present. So, in hopes of shaking them up, I spoke about utopia. I talked about the meaning of utopia, the value of utopian thinking, and attempts to create utopian communities. To my surprise, they responded enthusiastically. During the question and answer period, one student said, "Engineers are always trying to make things that don't exist. That's what we do."

I had wrongly expected the engineering students to be dismissive of utopian thinking—what is often disparaged as wishful thinking. "That's just pie in the sky" we hear in response to ideas for making new things, for solving problems that have stumped us for a long time, or for making the world a better place. This is often followed by stern advice to focus one's mind on down-to-earth, here-and-now realities and stop dreaming about things that will never be. Imagining how things could be different, we are thus taught, is a waste of time. The engineering students knew better.

It's a good thing, too, that many people throughout history have known better. We wouldn't have the world we have today if people before us hadn't imagined things that didn't yet exist: roads, canals, airplanes, cars, phones, computers, ships, televisions, vaccines; and also social constructions: laws, literature, symphonies, governments, hospitals, schools, banks, libraries, cities, nations, and so on. The technologies and social institutions that make our lives safe, interesting, and pleasurable exist because some people refused to stop their wishful thinking. Without the ability to imagine and a willingness to use that ability, we would be living, if we had survived at all, much like our chimpanzee cousins.

The external world can of course resist the realization of our imaginings. No matter how vividly you imagine being able to fly by flapping your arms, it won't happen. Likewise, the sincerest hope for a world without war won't bring about peace—not without action. But that is the point: imagining alone doesn't make things happen; rather, imagining guides the action that in turn transforms the world. Imagination is also subject to revision when the external world resists. If we can't fly by flapping our arms, maybe we can build a machine of some sort to carry us through the air.

All of us do a great deal of imagining as a natural part of being human. We do it when we make plans, when we empathize, when we rehearse conversations, when we reflect on the past, when we think about how our lives might be different if we had taken a different path, when we try to solve problems. It is this practice of imagining—working with mental representations of the external world—that enables us to transcend trial and error and generalize from experience. It's also what enables us to shape the world, not just be dragged along by it.

Despite the tendency to dismiss imagining as mere philosophizing or navel gazing, it is one of the most practical things we can do if we want to improve the world. We need visions of what solutions to social problems would look like and of what a better world would look like. We need them, as in other realms of human life, as inspirations and guides to action. And even people who itch to forgo philosophizing and jump straight into action are always operating with some imagined future in mind. Imagining, then, is not only practical but necessary for making change. I'm going to suggest that we can do it more usefully—for purposes of making change—if we treat imagining not just as something individuals do, but as a social practice.

Imagining as a Social Practice

Earlier I might have made it seem that this book is a product of nothing but my imagination. That's not true. Most of the ideas offered here come from long traditions of thought, developed over time by many people. And of course there would be no books in anyone's hands without people organized to edit, publish, print, market, and distribute them, as well as people organized to teach others to read. So creating this book depended on a great many conditions external to my imagination. In fact, without these conditions, I wouldn't have been able to imagine creating anything like a book.

The same is true of all human creating. To imagine and build a new machine or electronic device depends on a multitude of prior conditions being in place to make it possible. Even artists who seem to be gushing wells of creativity depend on others who make and sell materials, others who establish traditions (within which an artist might work or against which an artist might rebel), others who sell art, others who write about it, and others who buy it. Imagining and creating are, then, always parts of a process that occurs within a larger social world—one that extends far beyond the mind, workshop, or studio of a lone maker.

What does this have to do with making the world a better place? The point is this: we need to appreciate the social nature of imagining to best nurture it as part of making change. We also need to recognize that constructive social change can't occur without collective imagining. Here is what I mean.

By definition, social change means changing how we do things together. So while it's possible to sit alone in a dark room and imagine a new social world, this won't lead to change unless we connect our imaginings to those of other people. To do this, we need to draw on ideas created by others and also make our ideas sensible to others. Only in this way can others begin to see the value in what we imagine, only in this way can we see the limits of our ideas and go beyond those limits with the help of others, and only in this way can we begin to act in concert to turn imaginings into reality.

As individuals, we are free to imagine any kind of social worlds that occur to us. We can mentally craft whatever alternative realities we like. Writers of science fiction and fantasy do this, and sometimes their visions help us see how the current world is not the only possible world (or they might help us see how current social arrangements are leading us into trouble). In everyday life, even if we are not writers of science fiction and fantasy, we can do the same thing by asking, *How might we do things differently? What if we did things this way instead of that? If current trends continue, where will we end up?* Posing these questions to ourselves and others can put imagining to use in the process of creating a different world.

What I am proposing is that imagining, for purposes of social change, is best done collectively. By jointly creating a shared vision of a different way of doing things together, we can enrich that vision because it will reflect more ideas and perspectives. We also keep the vision tethered to reality—to real possibilities for change, not just fantasies—because when people co-construct a vision, they are more likely to embrace it and see it as worth trying. Collective imagining is also more likely to identify problems. What might seem like a brilliant solution from one perspective might be obviously flawed from another. Because social change depends on cooperation, the visions that will serve to guide and inspire change must be cooperatively constructed.

If the process I'm describing is not open to dissent, it can be disastrous. When individuals or small groups decide that everyone must accept their version of a better world without question or conversation, oppression can follow, especially if a group of true believers is able to wield power over others. Religious cults and fanatical political groups are classic examples. We should thus be wary of rigid plans for a new world advanced by leaders or groups who will brook no challenges to those plans. History has shown that imposed utopias usually turn out to be dystopias.

We often talk about imagination as a quality of mind that one possesses or not. But if we think of imagining as a practice, a form of doing, then it makes sense to think about how we can do it better or more often. In the next section, I'll suggest how we can do it better and more often, in more constructive ways, individually and collectively. If we want to make the world a better place, it helps to bring all our powers of mind to bear on the task, along with the powers of more minds. Here are some suggestions for how to do this.

Nurturing Practical Imagination

Although everyone is capable of imagining, some people are better at it than others. What do they do that others don't? It seems that people who are especially creative rely on a handful of techniques to generate ideas. These techniques alone won't turn a person into a creative artist. On the other hand, they can be used by anyone who wants to try to see beyond things as they are.

Explore counterfactuals. No one can run beside an advancing light beam. But if it were possible to do this, what would one see? Einstein used this thought experiment to develop his theory of relativity. We can all do the same sort of thing, stretching our minds by asking *What if?* questions. This kind of thinking can be helpful for understanding not only how the world works (as per Einstein) but also how it might work. For example, we might ask, What if public universities charged no tuition? It doesn't matter that free college education might seem impossible right now. By imagining the possibility we can begin to explore it, think about its costs and potential benefits, and then, if the benefits seem to outweigh the costs, begin to think about how to make it happen. What's important for pursuing change is to avoid letting defenders of the status quo stop imagination in its tracks by declaring things impossible before they have even been seriously considered.

Turn things upside down. Suppose you benefited greatly from the status quo and did not want to see it changed. Suppose, therefore, that you wanted to keep people from imagining alternatives. What would you do? How would you try to stamp out imagination? It might seem odd to pose these questions in a book about making change, but they're actually useful for that purpose. If we think about how to put an end to imagining—something that dictators and ruling elites might like to do—we can perhaps see better how to encourage it. If we consider how imagination might be quashed, we can gain insight into how it might be sparked. This is another kind of thought experiment to generate new ideas. Sometimes by imagining what we do not want to see happen, we can get a new perspective on what we want to make happen.

Reject conventional realism. Sometimes people who criticize the high degree of inequality in US society will soften their critique by saying, "Oh, but I'm not proposing that we eliminate inequality entirely." Well, why not? If inequality is a problem, why not at least imagine what a society would look like without it? Why not imagine a society without social classes? Why not imagine a society in which no one believes in the fiction of race? Or a society without gender? The point of imagining is to see new possibilities by getting beyond what we take for granted. If we remain attached to things that now seem inevitable—inequality, social class, race, gender—we might never see those possibilities. To make full use of imagination requires that we not let it be caged by conventional realism.

Imagine a process. Imagining an egalitarian society might help us conceive of it as a possibility, but at the same time it might seem so far from current reality that we can't imagine how to get there. Which again leaves us stuck in the present. So we might try a different kind of imagining, one that starts in the present and moves forward gradually. For example, we could look at current levels of inequality and imagine how things might be a little different, a little more equal. If we can imagine a little more equal world, we can take another step and imagine a world with still more equality, and a little more after that. If we can imagine these incremental changes, it becomes easier to imagine a process—a set of realistic, doable steps—through which they might be achieved. This is also part of the power of imagining: it allows us to see not only distant futures but also the path in front of us, on which we must take one step after another.

Seek models. Over the years, students have told me that the following things are impossible: workplace democracy, proportional representation in government, national health insurance, prisons that rehabilitate, and free higher education. While these might be nice ideas, some students have said, they could never work. In response, I have pointed out that these things have been realities for a long time in many places around the world. This is hard for some students to conceive because their imaginations have been arrested by the idea that There Is No Alternative (TINA) to what they have seen around them. One way to overcome this problem is to seek models, to look elsewhere to find out what others have done. These models can then be fuel for imagination—starting points for imagining practical solutions to problems that seem intractable until TINA thinking is overcome.

Try alternative perspectives. In sociology, students sometimes fall in love with a particular theorist and then try to use that theorist's ideas to explain everything. This is fine. It gives people a place to start making sense of things. But then I often recommend that they try looking at whatever they're studying from a radically different perspective. Doing this can jog the imagination and bring fresh ideas to mind. Trying out alternative perspectives doesn't mean adopting them (see what I said about the "believing game" in chapter 2). It means using them to see more complexity than we might see if we use only one perspective all the time. Everyone can do this sort of thing. It's usually possible by reading and talking to others—those who are likely to see the world in a way different from ours—to find alternative perspectives and use them to broaden our imagining.

Think analogically. Thinking analogically means trying to understand an unfamiliar thing in terms of a familiar thing (analogical thinking is similar to metaphorical thinking). For example, in trying to understand human social behavior, we might liken it to theater, to a market, or to a game. Or suppose we're trying to understand imagining.

We might liken it to conducting experiments in a mental laboratory before taking action in the real world. We can apply analogical thinking to anything we are trying to better understand. How does social change occur? Perhaps it is like a river carving out a canyon, or like the shifting of tectonic plates, or like a fire raging through a dry forest. Perhaps it is nothing like any of these things. The point is that playing with analogies can shake up our minds in ways that lead to fresh insights.

If imagining is a form of doing, we can train ourselves to do it better. We can try to turn the techniques I've described into habits of mind—make them part of how we usually think. This can boost our creativity as individuals and make us better problem-solvers in everyday life. But we can do even more by making these techniques part of how we collaborate to solve problems. When we bounce ideas off each other, they often stick together in surprising new ways or break apart into surprising new forms. This is the process through which we can discover more possible futures than any of us might have discovered alone.

Conditions for Collective Imagining

Earlier I proposed imagining what it would take to stop people from thinking about social change. It would probably be impossible to do this entirely; no matter how oppressed people might be, they can usually imagine, in the safety of their minds, what relief from oppression would look like. Even so, clever tyrants could try to keep a lid on disruptive imagining. One strategy would be to punish people who expressed unorthodox ideas. People could be arrested, imprisoned, killed, fired from their jobs, or ridiculed. This would send a message to others to keep their minds offline and their mouths shut.

It's not necessary to beat people down or deprive them of their livelihood to discourage imagining. In fact, harsh strategies often backfire because they make people angry and eager for change. A better strategy is to convince people that imagining a different world is pointless. This might be done through schooling that discredits or ignores alternatives, or that teaches people to see the status quo as made by God or nature and therefore inevitable. Again, if people can be convinced, gently and invisibly, that there is no alternative to current social arrangements, then they are less likely to imagine what a different future might look like.

The point of thinking about how to dampen imagination, as I suggested earlier, is to think about how to spark it. If it's possible to create conditions that impede imagining, then it's possible to create conditions that encourage it. For example, laws and policies that protect dissent and free speech (see chapter 10) can help to encourage imagining by making people free to do it without fear—or with less fear—of being punished by those in power. Another strategy is to educate people about past and present alternatives to the status quo. This strategy can be built into schooling, as can attention to a wide range of ideas.

The condition that is perhaps most conducive to imagining is democracy. When people participate as equals in running the groups, organizations, and societies in which they live, they have incentive to imagine new possibilities and share their ideas—to put them on the table for others to consider. Democratic dialogue can, in turn, fuel both individual and collective imagining, as more ideas enter and enrich the conversation. So if we want to nurture imagination, we might begin by imagining how to create less hierarchy and more democracy in everyday life.

I have been writing about imagining as if it were always done to serve the common good. Unfortunately, it isn't. Imagining can be the precursor to creating terrible as well as wonderful things. Imagining can also paralyze us, if we imagine that trying to change things is futile or likely to be ruinous. And in a world where exploitation and inequality are still seen as acceptable, imagining always carries the risk that it will be used to enhance exploitation and increase inequality. So by itself imagining doesn't necessarily make the world better.

What matters is what we do with our capacity to imagine. Yes, we can imagine nightmarish futures, but such possibilities should warn us, not paralyze us. As in using imagination to solve any kind of problem, we want to use it to avoid, if we can, creating worse problems. But if we don't imagine, if we don't nurture this capacity of our minds, then we fail to make use of the greatest power to make constructive change that humans possess. The risks of disaster are greater, I would say, if we don't use the imaginative power of more minds to solve our shared problems.

Imagining that we are powerless to make change is what really paralyzes us, more so than dystopian nightmares. Imagining that there is nothing we can do leaves us doing nothing. But there is plenty we can do to make the world a better place. We don't have to lead a revolution or single-handedly change the world through acts of moral heroism. The reality is more mundane. We can listen, teach, write, organize, research, empathize, advocate, conserve, and dissent. If we do these doable things, we can make a difference and help create the better world that we imagine.

To Learn More

Asma, Stephen T. (2017). *The Evolution of Imagination*. Chicago: University of Chicago Press.

Becker, Howard S. (1982). *Art Worlds*. Chicago: University of Chicago Press.

Fuentes, Agustin. (2017). *The Creative Spark: How Imagination Made Humans Exceptional*. New York: Dutton.

John-Steiner, Vera. (2000). *Creative Collaboration*. New York: Oxford University Press.

Lakoff, George, and Johnson, Mark. (2003). *Metaphors We Live By*. Chicago: University of Chicago Press.

Mulgan, Geoff. (2018). *Big Mind: How Collective Intelligence Can Change Our World*. Princeton, NJ: Princeton University Press.

Ofshe, Richard. (1977). *The Sociology of the Possible* (2nd ed.). Englewood Cliffs, NJ: Prentice-Hall.

Reich, Brian. (2017). *The Imagination Gap*. Bingley, UK: Emerald Publishing.

Rigney, Daniel. (2001). *The Metaphorical Society*. Lanham, MD: Rowman and Littlefield.

Sloman, Steven, and Fernbach, Philip. (2017). *The Knowledge Illusion: Why We Never Think Alone*. New York: Riverhead Books.

Wilson, Edward O. (2017). *The Origins of Creativity*. New York: Liveright Publishing.

CHAPTER 12

A Sociologically Mindful Path
to Social Change

When I look at the social world, I see a need for repair. There are laws and policies that don't produce the results they should; instead of reducing inequality and suffering, they make these problems worse. There are class systems that cause tremendous waste of human potential. There is heedlessness to environmental destruction and alteration of the earth's climate. There is tribalism that needlessly pits people against each other.

I see other problems. Government agencies that are supposed to protect us from abuse by the powerful often fail to do so. Corporations that are supposed to abide by rules intended to protect workers and consumers often break or ignore these rules, causing much harm. Organizations that are supposed to fairly distribute opportunities to get ahead often don't. Governments that are supposed to be democratic drift toward authoritarianism. When I see all this, it occurs to me that we have a great deal of repair work to do.

My analogy between repair and social change isn't perfect. People and organizations aren't machines. We can't just spot loose wires or worn gears and step in with a one-person fix. Social change means changing how we do things together, and this in turn means that social change always requires striving for mutual understanding and cooperation, while posing risks of misunderstanding and conflict. For this kind of repair, we need an approach, a way of seeing, that attunes us to how the social world works. That approach is what I have been calling sociological mindfulness.

In chapter 1, I described five aspects of sociological mindfulness that are most relevant to pursuing change: awareness of the social world as humanly made; awareness of interdependence; awareness of the social bases of power; awareness of inequality and connections between multiple forms of inequality; and awareness of social life as a process. By paying attention to these matters, we can see what must be taken into account if we want to try to move the world in the direction of democracy, peace, and justice.

Some readers might see sociological mindfulness as just a form of heightened awareness. I suppose it could be taken this way; being sociologically mindful is not the same as being engaged with other people in efforts to make change. Yet throughout this book, I have tied sociological mindfulness to actions one can take to make a difference. I have also tried, in every chapter, to offer practical advice that follows from or is consistent with being sociologically mindful. Although not a complete guide to repairing the world, *Making a Difference* offers plenty of tips for getting started.

Other readers might think that I should have addressed specific issues or current policy debates. There are three reasons why I haven't done this. One reason is that the issues that seem pressing to me might not be pressing to others, and I don't want readers to think that making a positive difference requires accepting my priorities. A second reason is that I think readers can find ways to apply my advice to the change-making efforts that matter to them. The third reason is that I think the way forward needs to be discovered together, not prescribed by teachers or gurus.

To return to my repair analogy: what I have described in this book are practices through which we can all help repair and rebuild the social world. These practices don't require genius, moral heroism, or celebrity status. Nor do they require pursuing a career as an activist, professor, or politician. Everyone reading this book can do some or all of the things I've suggested: listening, organizing, writing, researching, teaching, empathizing, advocating, conserving, dissenting, imagining. If you want to help make the world a better place, these are the ways to do it. Start wherever there is work to be done, as the spirit so moves you.

Before tackling this final chapter, I reread the preceding ones. I tried to think of questions about social change that I raised but didn't answer. I also looked for principles that are hidden between the lines, so to speak, and that might be worth drawing out more sharply. In the remaining pages, I'll try to tie up these loose ends. I'll also say why I think being sociologically mindful helps us see not only problems but also a kind of beauty in social life, beauty that can be a source of optimism.

A Continuum of Change

Much of the advice I've offered might seem more useful for pursuing reforms than for overhauling dominant social institutions, especially government and the economy. A skeptical reader might say that more awareness or compassion would be nice, and maybe this would make life more pleasant for some people, but that solving our problems will require radical changes in how major societal institutions operate. For the most part, I agree.

Capitalism can't be reformed to generate equality, or even equality of opportunity. The concentrations of wealth and power that capitalism inevitably creates are antithetical to democracy. Authoritarian bureaucracies are prone to corruption. Hierarchy inherently fuels competition and strife. As long as we're stuck with these arrangements, we're going to have to deal with the problems that arise from them.

So I am sympathetic to the view that heightened social consciousness, more mindfulness, and modest reforms are not enough. Creating a world free from exploitation, injustice, and violence will require radical change in the long run, not just a tweak here and there. Yet I would say that local, small-scale change, what might seem like mere reform, should be appreciated as part of the process by which more profound change is achieved.

Here is an example (similar to one I used in chapter 5). Suppose you are tired of being mistreated by an employer. You'd like to change the situation but you know that alone you don't have much power; your complaints won't matter—you can either keep suffering or quit. But then it occurs to you that if you organize your co-workers and confront the employer together, you might be able to get the change you're seeking. So how do you proceed?

You could use the strategies I described in chapter 5 on organizing. But you'd probably need to do other things as well: listening, teaching, writing, empathizing, researching, dissenting, advocating, imagining.

If you were able to form a strong employees' group—call it a union or whatever you like—you could perhaps compel the employer, under threat of a strike or bad publicity, to act differently. The change you achieve might not be earth-shaking; it might be only reform in one workplace, but it's real change nonetheless.

Now imagine that workers elsewhere are inspired by your example and begin to organize in their workplaces. If this were to happen, the change you achieved locally could have much wider effects. A next step would be for all the worker organizations to form a coalition and try to change laws or elect more worker-friendly (instead of employer-friendly) representatives. This still wouldn't amount to an overhaul of the economy. But new laws that expanded workers' rights could tip the balance of power enough to enable further change.

Maybe at some point you realize that the change you want is impossible within a system that gives owners and bosses ultimate control over the workplace and over most of society's economic resources. Now you might decide to create worker-owned and worker-controlled enterprises. Or you might decide to try transforming government to make it more democratic, so that you can use it to reduce the power of bosses and owners to dictate the conditions of life for everyone else. Such a project, if it succeeded, would indeed amount to a radical change in how society operates.

Although this example is hypothetical, it alludes to how real social movements begin and grow. People in one place get tired of being treated unfairly; they question the social arrangements that have been imposed on them; they imagine and talk about alternatives; they try to figure out what needs to be done and how to do it; they act collectively, learning and adapting as they go along; and then people elsewhere, people who experience similar problems, see the example and emulate it. When local struggles inspire other local struggles, and when these struggles begin to flow together, large-scale change can occur.

What I'm getting at is this: the change-making practices I've recommended can produce more than reforms. They are the same practices needed to make change on any scale. In the modern world, any serious effort to change laws, organizations, or institutions will require listening, empathizing, researching, writing, teaching, organizing, advocating, dissenting, and imagining. Whether the house we're trying to repair or rebuild is large or small, we need the same tools and skills.

Today, we can communicate and coordinate action quickly across great distances, thus creating the sense that we can "act globally" rather than just locally. But all change must begin where people live, where they suffer, where they meet and share ideas, and where they try to help each other break from the routine patterns of behavior that reproduce the status quo. For change to happen on any scale, people must be willing to depart from the paths of least resistance that they walk in everyday life. If we can join this process of change in one place, using the tools of sociological mindfulness, we can potentially contribute to its unfolding everywhere.

Principles to Guide the Practices

In the preceding chapters, I offered a lot of advice about how to pursue change in a sociologically mindful way. I focused on doable things such as listening, writing, organizing, researching, and so on. But it occurred to me, as I reread what I'd written, that I had left unspoken some key principles concerning social change, activism, and intellectual life. Articulating these principles will be helpful, I hope, for encouraging sociological mindfulness and mindful engagement in the pursuit of social change.

Knowledge is tested and refined in action. We learn from what we read, hear, and see. In school, much weight is put on reading books and listening to teachers. But it's also important to learn from experience, especially when it comes to social change. It's always necessary to figure out which ideas work and which don't, under the circumstances we face. Ideas that work—ideas that effectively guide action—should be kept. Those that don't work should be revised or put on the shelf. This is what it means to test and refine knowledge in action. It is through this process of putting ideas into practice that we gain power to make sense of the social world and to change it. If we don't embrace this process, we may end up with many elegant ideas of little practical value.

Passion is not fanaticism. Working for change always entails some discomfort, if only because it means confronting others who don't want the boat rocked. A willingness to carry on despite this discomfort usually comes from a passion for justice or for reducing the suffering of others. It's hard to sustain commitment to change without such passion. But fanaticism goes too far. Fanaticism takes the form of believing that one has found the truth, that no other perspectives are valid, that no new ideas are worth considering, and that opposition must be overcome at all costs by any means necessary. When fanaticism takes hold, the result is almost always more tyranny, conflict, and violence. Passion in the service of justice and equality can make the world a better place, whereas fanaticism is likely to perpetuate existing problems or make them worse.

Analysis is more productive than blame. When we look at social problems, we often think like prosecutors, looking for villains who can be blamed. Sometimes this is necessary; people who knowingly harm others should be held accountable for their misdeeds. But a prosecutorial way of thinking can blind us to the social conditions, social processes, laws and policies, and institutional routines that generate patterns of harmful behavior—despite people's conscious intentions. If our interest is in change, then we need to move beyond blame. If we can see how social problems arise from the ways in which we do things together, we will have a much better chance of seeing what needs to be changed to produce better results.

Self-change is part of social change. How does it occur to us that we don't have to obey and conform? How does it occur to us to imagine and explore alternatives to the status quo? To reach this point requires internal changes that grow out of self-reflection. This kind of individual-level change is sometimes dismissed as psychological and unimportant for social change. But in fact, individual change and social change are connected. If social change means changing how we do things together, we have to change ourselves—by reflecting on our beliefs, values, and desires and by acquiring new skills—so as to become ready and able to try new ways of doing things together. When we do this, when we step off the path of least resistance, we learn new things that can further transform us. Self-change and social change are thus inseparable.

Problems can't be solved unless they're faced. No doubt this seems like a truism. I state it here because of the natural tendency to turn away from what makes us uncomfortable. This tendency is evident when people fault sociology for calling problems to our attention. But how can we solve problems if we don't face them? Finding solutions also requires a willingness to act, and what usually moves us to act is the suffering we experience when we are treated unjustly or we see others being treated unjustly. To get to this point—the point of readiness to act—requires that we honestly confront problems and the suffering they cause in ourselves and others. To turn away is to give up our power to make a difference.

Change requires balancing action and reflection. Reflection is important for self-change, for weighing ideas, for analyzing the social world, and for imagining alternative futures. But to make change, reflection must be turned into action. While it might seem obvious to say that both action and reflection are needed to make constructive social change, the two often get out of balance. The desire for action can make reflection seem like a waste of time. On the other hand, the safety and pleasure of reflection can be seductive and lead to postponing action until every last question is answered. There is no easy solution to this problem. We can only remain aware that reflection without action accomplishes little, and that action without reflection often makes matters worse. We need both to reflect and to act, in balance, using each kind of experience to inform the other.

Opportunities for change are always present. Responding to the demands of daily life can keep us busy. And so we often say, "I'm swamped. I just can't get involved right now." Such a statement reflects a belief that change can be made only by devoting a lot of time to a major organizing campaign. But opportunities to effect change are all around us. We can listen and empathize when others are suffering; we can teach by example; we can write or sign letters to oppose harmful inequalities; we can vocally or financially support those who lack power and are seeking justice; we can refuse to join in practices that demean others. These acts don't take much time; and while they might seem small, each act moves the world in a better direction. We can always find ways to nudge it along.

Commitment to change is sustained by relationships. Just as excessive busyness can interfere with working for change, so can feeling alone or unsupported in our efforts. Challenging the status quo can be emotionally tiring and lead to burnout. This is why relationships and communities are crucial for sustaining commitment to working for change. The energy and enthusiasm necessary to carry on the work comes from friends and colleagues who encourage us and join us in seeking change. Our support gives them strength as well. Nurturing these relationships is important not only for our own well-being, it's also part of how we change the larger social world.

Making the world a better place is a long process, one that we can take part in actively and wisely but never fully control or foresee. This is daunting, but it needn't be overwhelming. If we know which practices are effective (see chapters 2–11), we can choose to mindfully engage in these practices in ways that best suit our lives. If we are also aware of basic principles of social change, as I've articulated here, we can do more. We can use these principles like compass points to help us find and stay on a path to making a difference, even when we all we can see is the next step.

Optimism in a Troubled World

One time, years ago, when a student said in class that studying sociology is depressing because it points out so many problems in society, I responded with mock surprise. "What did you say?" I began. "*Sociology* is depressing? You must be forgetting your literature classes. If you want to be depressed, study Shakespeare. Take *Macbeth*, for example." This got everyone's attention. Students could tell that I was winding up to something.

Most students had read *Macbeth* in high school, or they at least knew the story. I reminded them of Macbeth's bloody rise to power and how, near the end of the play, his enemies are closing in and his kingdom is near collapse. And then his wife, wracked by guilt and losing her mind, kills herself. I recited (with thanks to my most demanding high school English teacher) Macbeth's soliloquy in scene 5 of act 5, delivered right after he learns of his wife's death:

> She should have died hereafter;
> There would have been a time for such a word.
> To-morrow, and to-morrow, and to-morrow,
> Creeps in this petty pace from day to day
> To the last syllable of recorded time,
> And all our yesterdays have lighted fools

The way to dusty death. Out, out, brief candle!
Life's but a walking shadow, a poor player
That struts and frets his hour upon the stage
And then is heard no more: it is a tale
Told by an idiot, full of sound and fury,
Signifying nothing.

"Now *that's* depressing," I said. There were a few laughs, but mostly silent stares, as if I'd gone off the rails. "Okay, seriously," I said, switching back to professor mode, "given that Shakespeare's depictions of human greed, corruptibility, and violence are more vivid than anything sociology gives us, why doesn't studying Shakespeare drive us to depression and despair?" It took a while to get there, but finally someone said that Shakespeare also shows us what's good and noble in human beings, and this gives us cause for hope. I said that sociology could show us this, too, albeit in a different way.

The Shakespeare ploy wasn't entirely spontaneous. I'd used it before, so I knew where I wanted to take the discussion and the points I wanted to make.

Yes, I said, sociology often highlights social problems, and this in itself isn't uplifting. In fact, it's reasonable to feel disheartened by a steady diet of bad news. But that's not all that sociology offers, I went on. Sociology also shows us how the social world is humanly made, how we create culture and routine ways of doing things together. This means that we have the power to remake the social world. It also means that the problems we create for ourselves are within our power to solve. Understanding this, and appreciating the tools for analysis that sociology gives us, ought to warrant some optimism—like the optimism we can take from Shakespeare when he shows us the kindness, strength, and courage that humans are capable of.

Being painfully aware of my poor skills as an actor, I don't do Shakespeare in class anymore. But I have thought more about how sociological mindfulness can help us see not only problems and suffering arising from how the social world works. It can also help us see more fully the prospects for creating a better world. Sociological mindfulness, then, can give us reasons for optimism.

Earlier I said that I see a world in need of repair. But this is not all I see. I also see the constructedness of the social world and the possibilities this implies for repair and rebuilding. I see complex systems of human cooperation and our abilities to accomplish amazing things together. I see how cooperation can generate mutual understanding and overcome tribalism. I see generosity and ingenuity in how we collaborate to nurture each new generation.

I see, too, the power of collective thinking in our abilities to analyze the world around us and imagine alternatives to the status quo. I see how excellence in human endeavors results from learnable skills and practices. I see people organizing to resist oppression and inequality. I see social life as a process, one that we can all influence, sometimes in surprising ways, through our chosen actions. To adapt a line from Charles Darwin, there is beauty and grandeur in this sociologically mindful view of human social life.

Shakespeare shows us how people can make a mess of things. And if all we had from him were the tragedies, the human condition would indeed appear bleak. But Shakespeare shows us much more. He also shows us how our capacities for love, sacrifice, wisdom, and solidarity can put things right, or at least give us the potential to do so. Looking at the world in a sociologically mindful way, we can see the same things— problems, yes, but also our potential to question, reflect, cooperate, imagine, and make change. In this there is reason for optimism that we can create a better world. We just have to find, each of us, our path to making a difference.

ACKNOWLEDGMENTS

....

Although I wasn't always thankful in the moment, I'm thankful now to all the students who ever asked how to solve the problems that sociology brings to light. If not for that persistent questioning, this book would not exist. The lesson for current readers is to keep asking hard, even irritating questions. That's how we find the limits of our knowledge and push ourselves to learn more.

Academics usually thank other academics, the met and unmet colleagues who read and comment on our writing. I'll do this, too. But first I want to thank a nonacademic group. These are the organizers and activists with whom I've worked and from whom I've learned over the years. If not for their wisdom, I would have had less to say about organizing and about how to balance theory and practice while seeking social change.

When I began writing *Making a Difference*, I had hoped to have the benefit of comments from my friend and colleague Allan Johnson. Some readers will recognize his name. Allan's best-known books—*The Forest and the Trees*, *The Gender Knot*, and *Privilege, Power, and Difference*—are models of how to write incisive and engaging sociology. Sadly, Allan died in December of 2017, before I could seek his counsel on the manuscript. I am grateful, though, to have had Allan's voice in my head as I struggled to say what I wanted to say as clearly as he would have said it.

Happily, I am able to thank another friend and colleague, Peter Callero, for his reading of the manuscript and encouragement. Peter, too, sets high standards when it comes to clarity and analytic acumen. His is another voice in my head that I am grateful to have. I hope that this book makes as much difference in the lives of readers as I know Peter's books have made.

Valuable input also came from those who served as reviewers for Oxford University Press. For help in making this a better book, my thanks to Tennille Allen (Lewis University), Patricia E. Carson (SUNY Suffolk County Community College), Sydney Hart (Wilbur Wright College), Austin H. Johnson (Kenyon College), Laura D. Lane-Worley (Lee College), Justin A. Martin (University of Tennessee at Martin), Reto Muller (East Stroudsburg University), Shaneel Pratap (San Jose City College), Matt Reid (Grand Valley State University), Jennifer Snook (Grinnell College), and Robert Wonser (College of the Canyons).

Some people can write productively in ten- or fifteen-minute sessions snatched here and there from the flow of a busy workday. Good for them. I need longer stretches of time and a more consistent schedule, both of which were afforded by a scholarly leave from North Carolina State University (NCSU) in the spring of 2018. Thanks to my department head, Bill Smith, and to the NCSU College of Humanities and Social Sciences for supporting my efforts.

Making a Difference is the third book—along with *The Sociologically Examined Life* and *Rigging the Game*—on which I've worked with my editor at Oxford University Press, Sherith Pankratz. On each occasion, Sherith has supported my vision, taken my writerly concerns seriously, and handled the vicissitudes of the publishing process with warmth and humor. Two thousand years ago I would have sacrificed a ram to the gods of publishing. Today, I hope my deepest thanks will suffice.

Most of what is said in the foregoing chapters was deliberated, at one time or another, with my life partner Sherryl Kleinman. For close to thirty years, we've joined in trying to make sense of the world sociologically, seeking ways to use the perspectives and lessons of sociology to make the world a better place. If this book makes a difference, it will be because of what she has helped me see and say. I would not have found this path without her.

INDEX

....

action
    for change, 34, 125
    collective, 34, 76–77, 120
    from imagining, 110
    from knowledge, 123
    physical, 90–91
    for problem solving, 124–25
active listening
    without advice, 20
    attention in, 19–21
    about diversity, 18
    fear related to, 17
    beyond hearing, 22–23
    judgment and, 20
    learning from, 18
    obstacles to, 17
    paraphrase related to, 20–21
    questions in, 20–21
    to whole message, 21
activism, 1. *See also specific topics*
adult achievement, 6
advocating. *See also* sociologically
        mindful advocacy
    allies and, 71–72
    through collective action, 76–77
    description of, 71

education related to, 70–71
    examples of, 72–73
    with others, 71–72, 76–77
    power and, 69–70, 107
    as teaching, 77, 88
allies, 54, 71–72
    co-workers as, 121–22
    sociologically mindful advocacy
        and, 73–74
alternative perspectives, 29–30, 115
analogical thinking, 115–16
analysis, 60–62, 124
anecdotal observation, 30
argument, 40–41, 103–4
assumptions examination, 32–33
attention, 11, 13, 52, 66
    in active listening, 19–21
    in listening, 21, 24
    in sociologically mindful
        teaching, 89
awareness, 95–96, 120

beliefs, 8–9. *See also* public writing
    in dissenting, 107
    questions about, 92
believing game, 23–24, 40

131